TIK-TOK OF OZ

ILLUSTRATED BY

JOHN R. NEILL

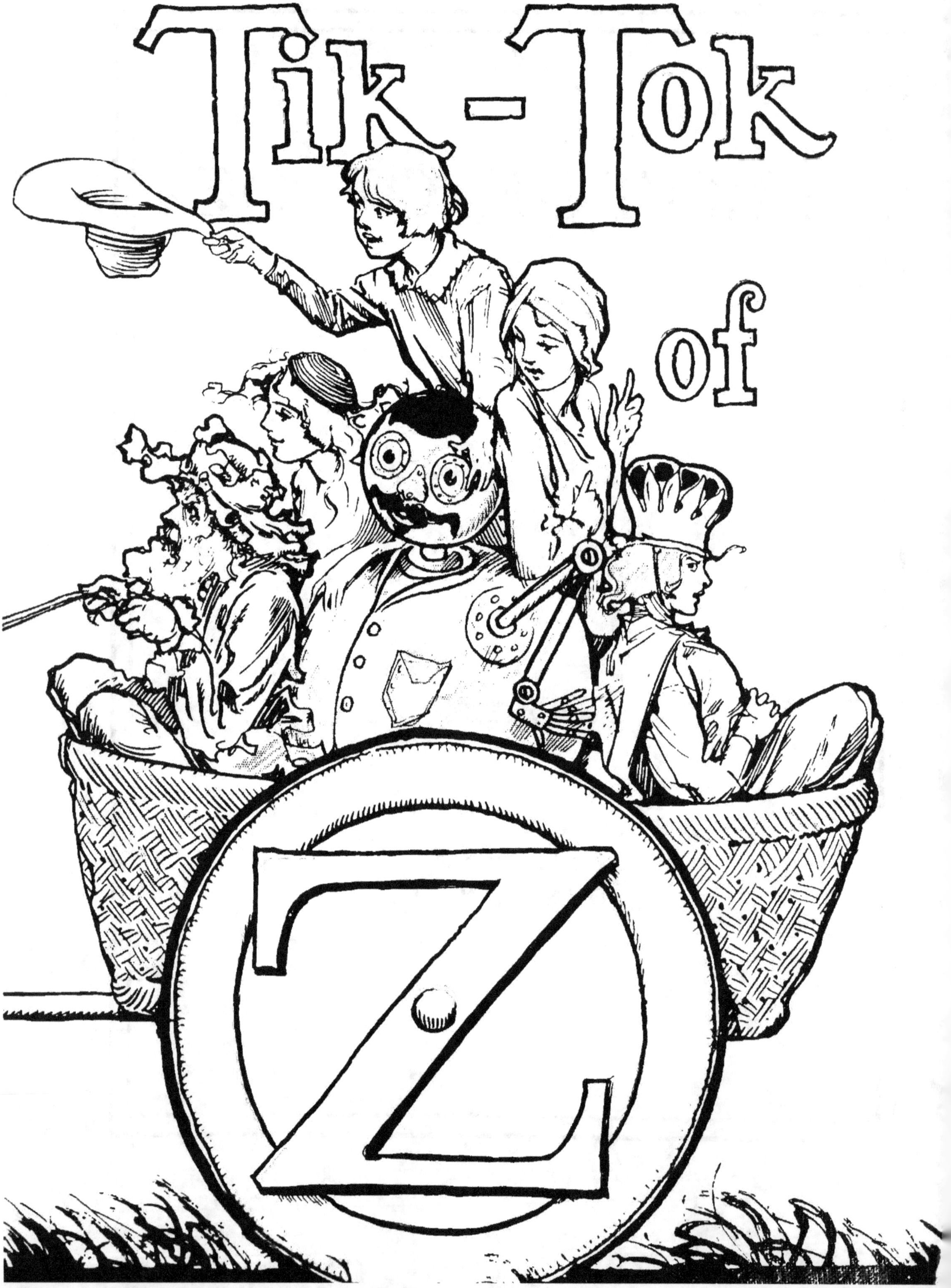
Tik-Tok of Oz

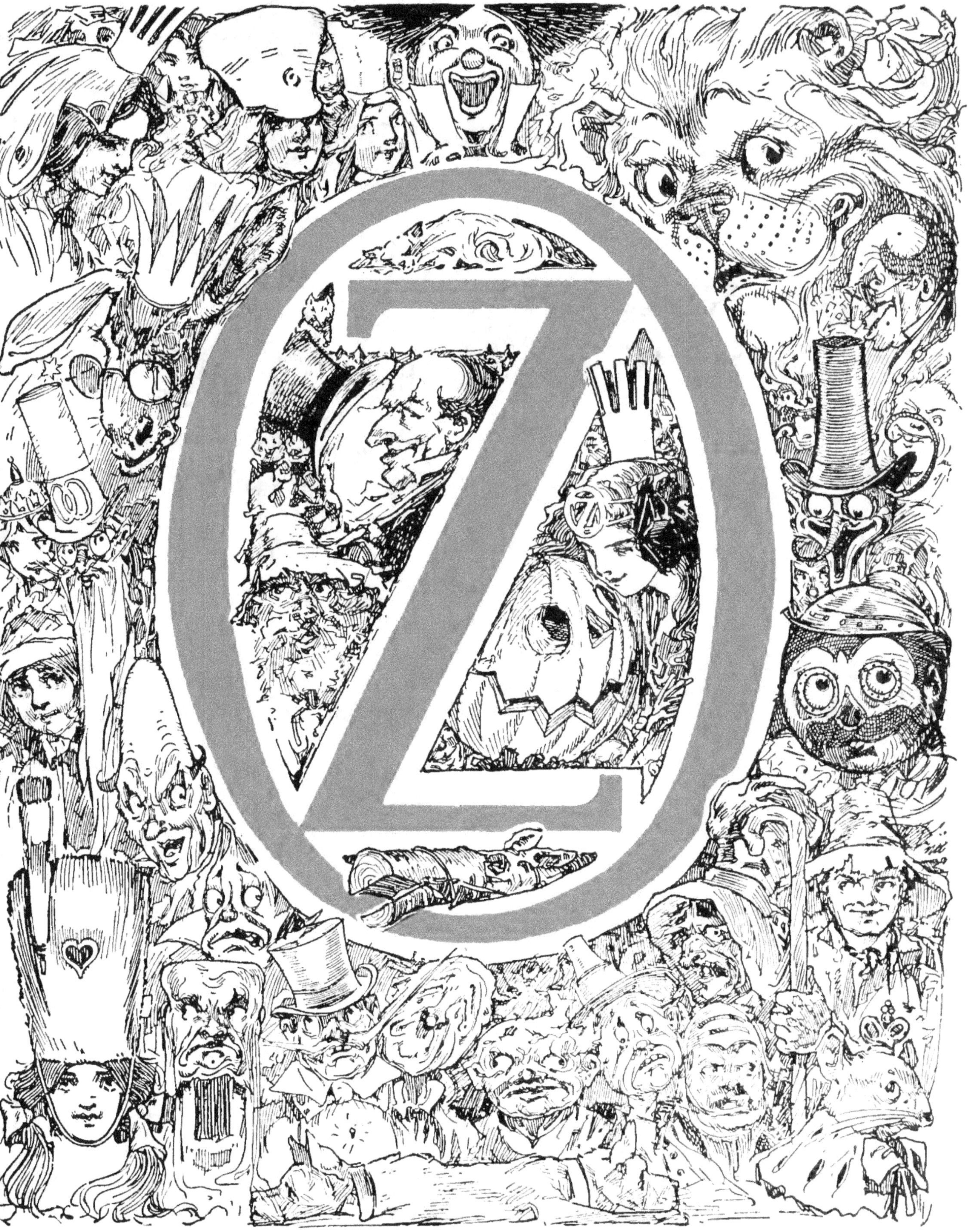

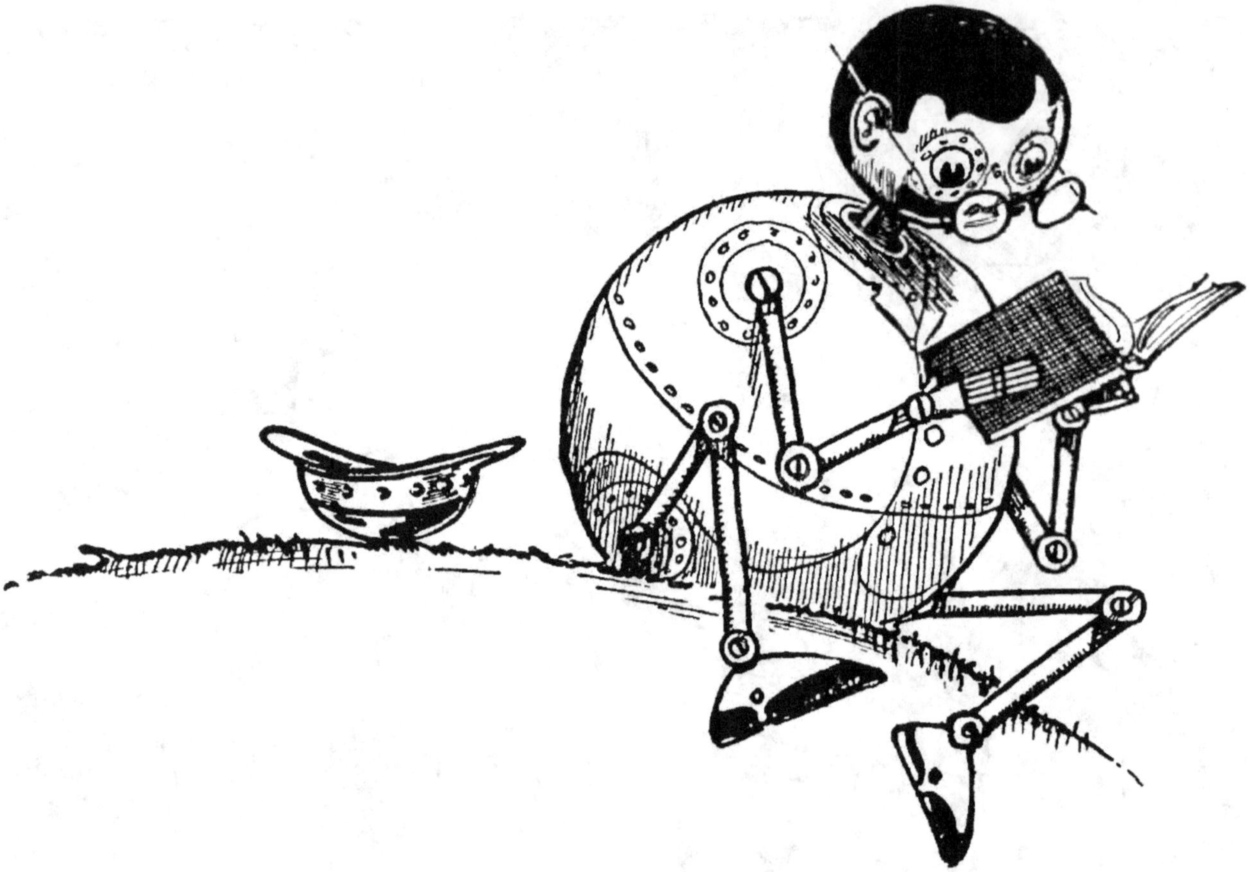

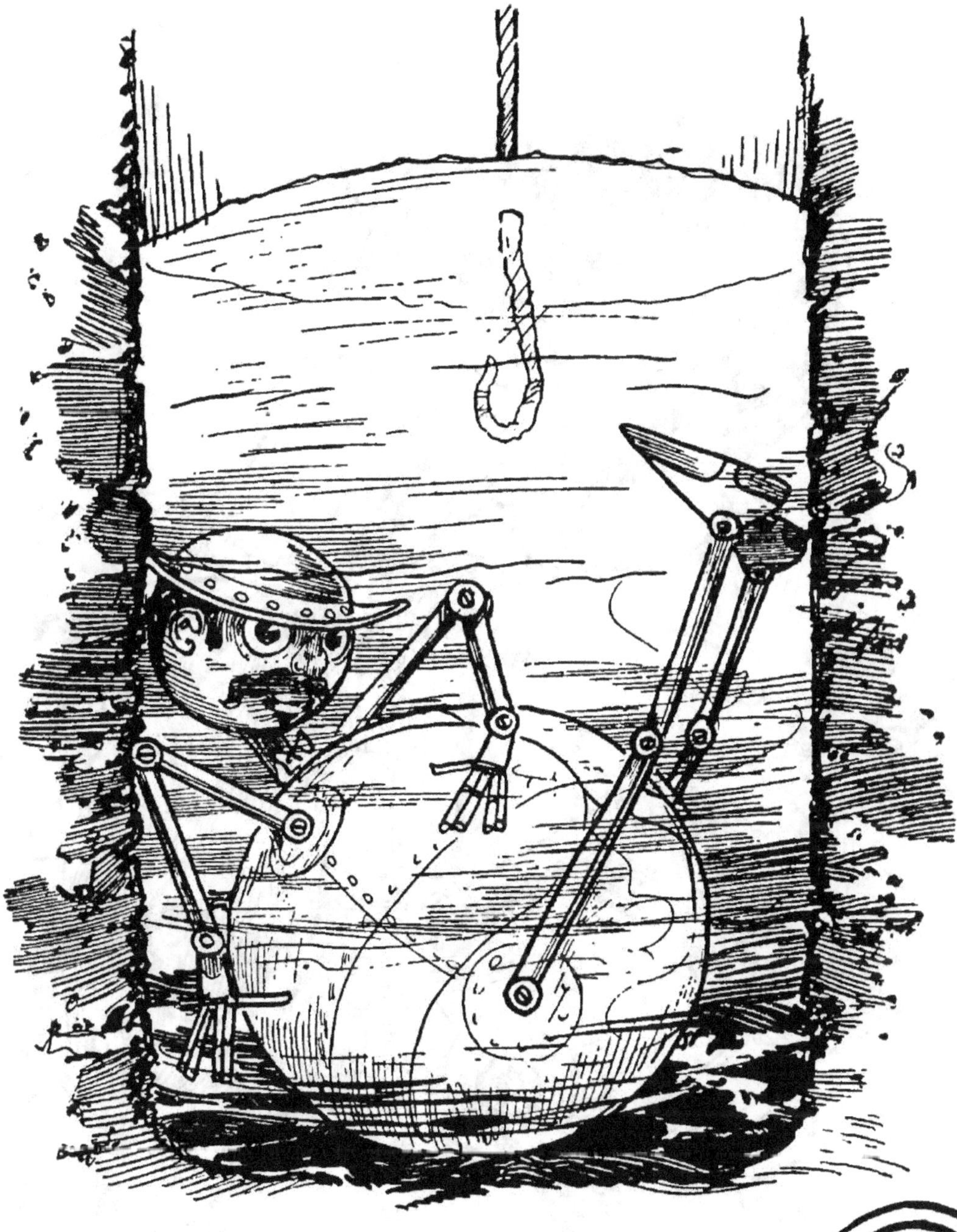

Tik-Tok of Oz

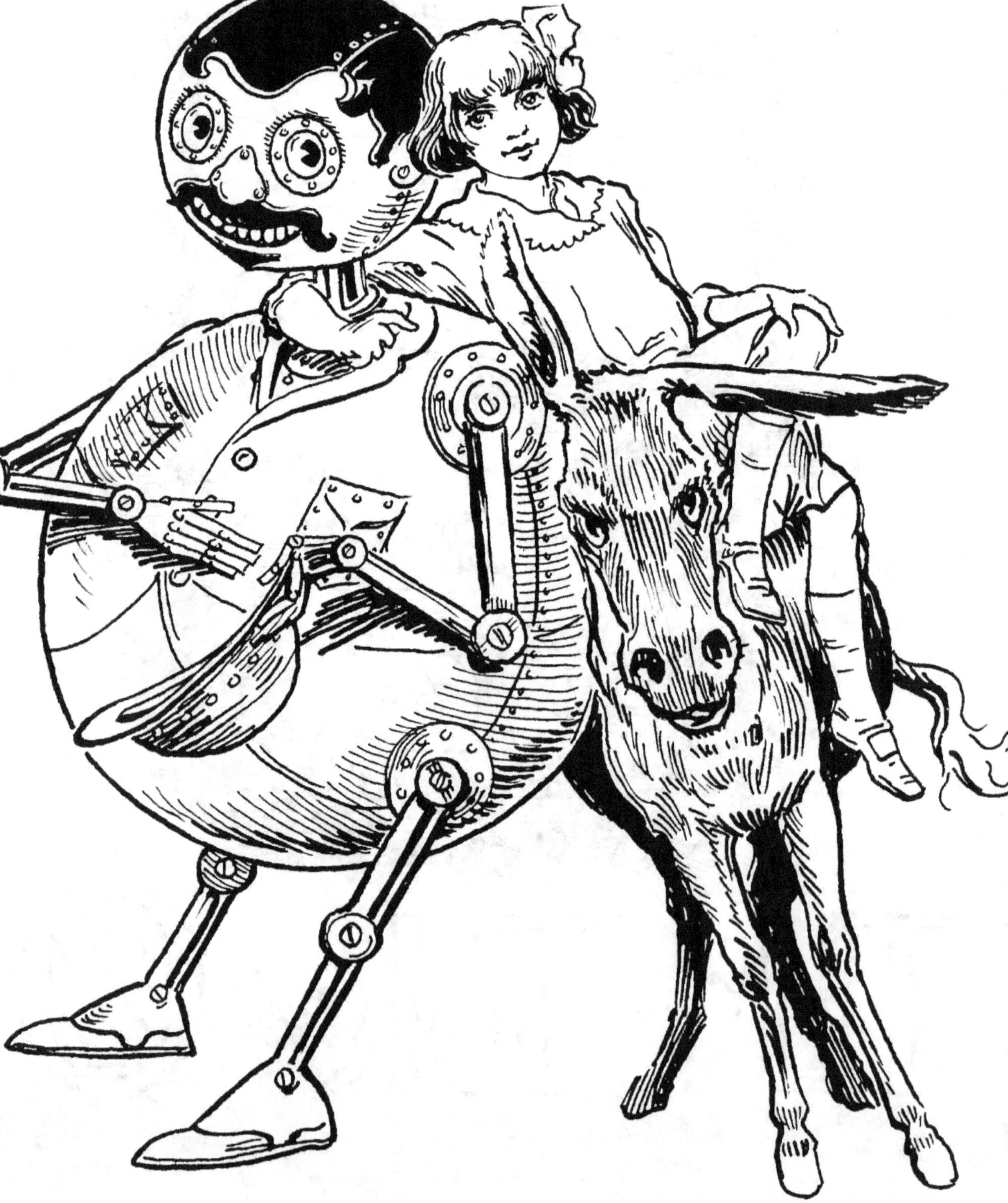

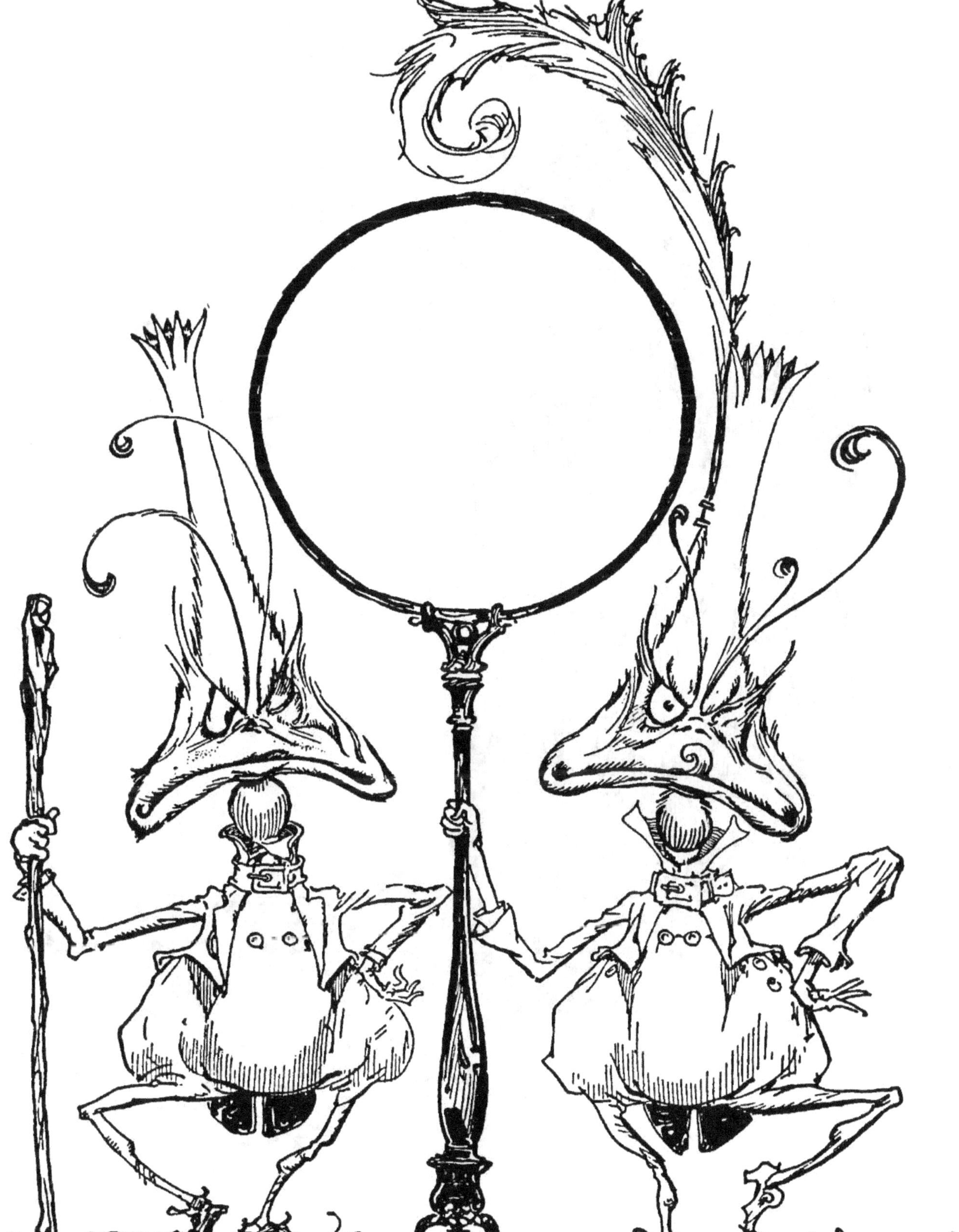

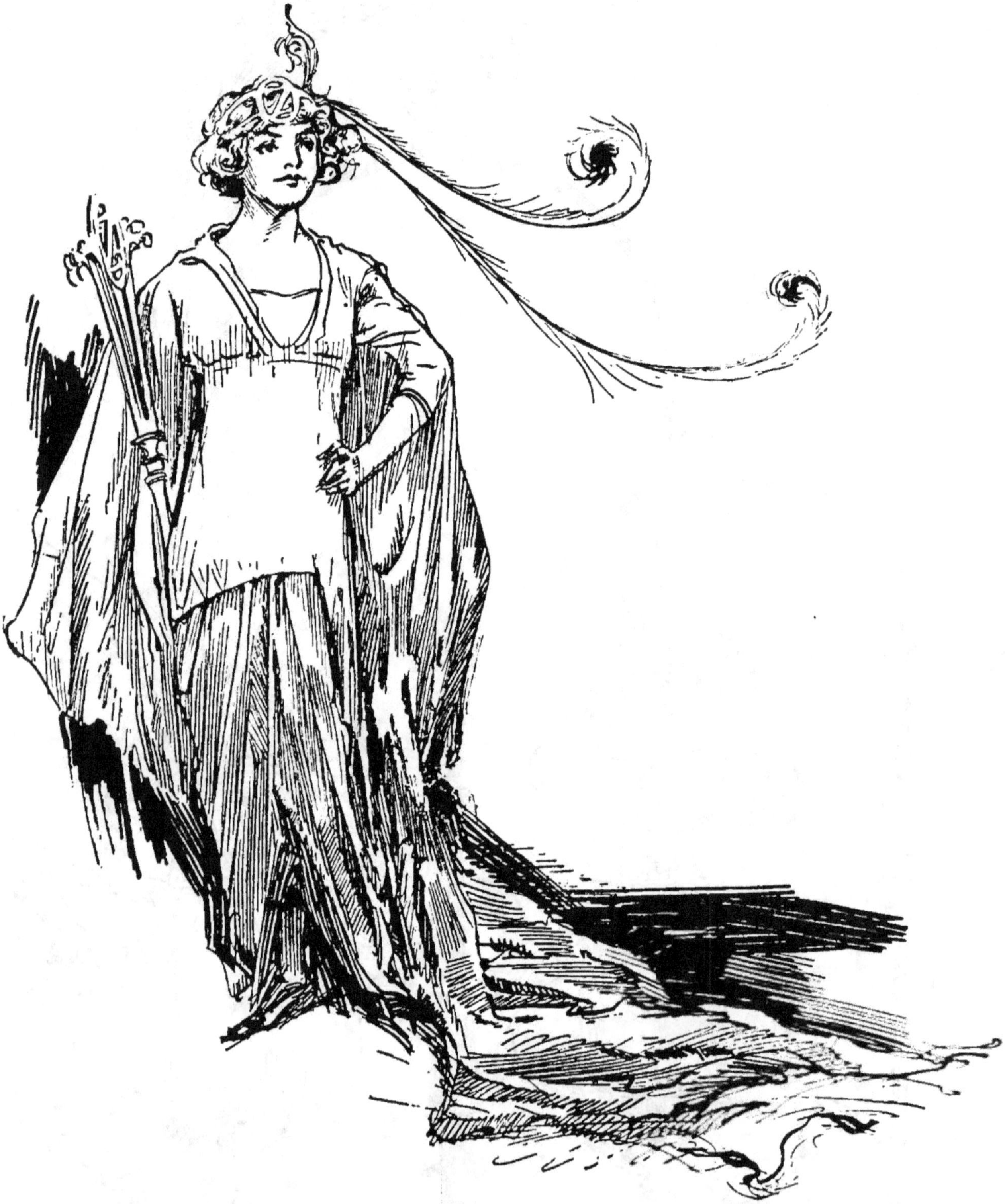

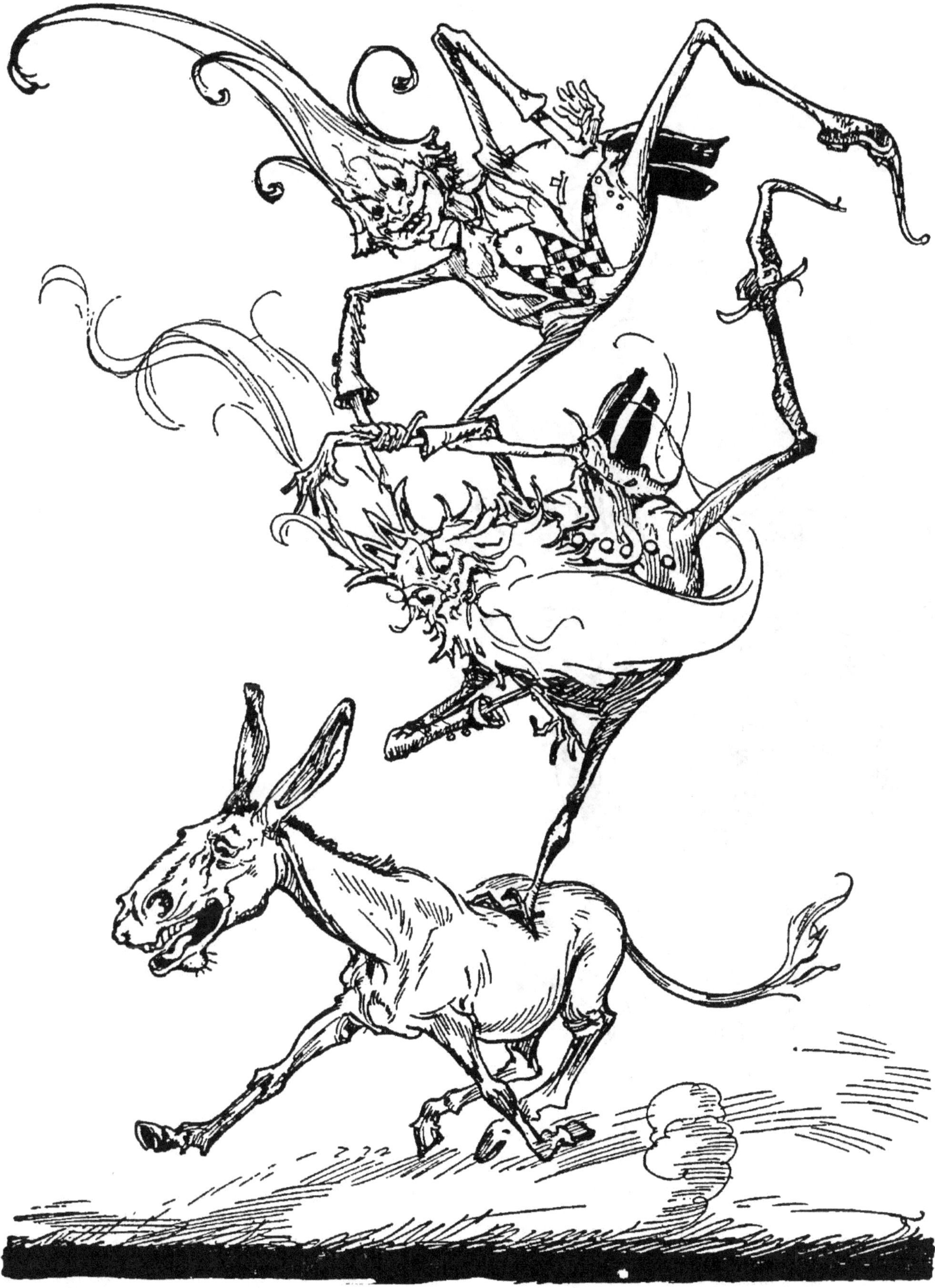

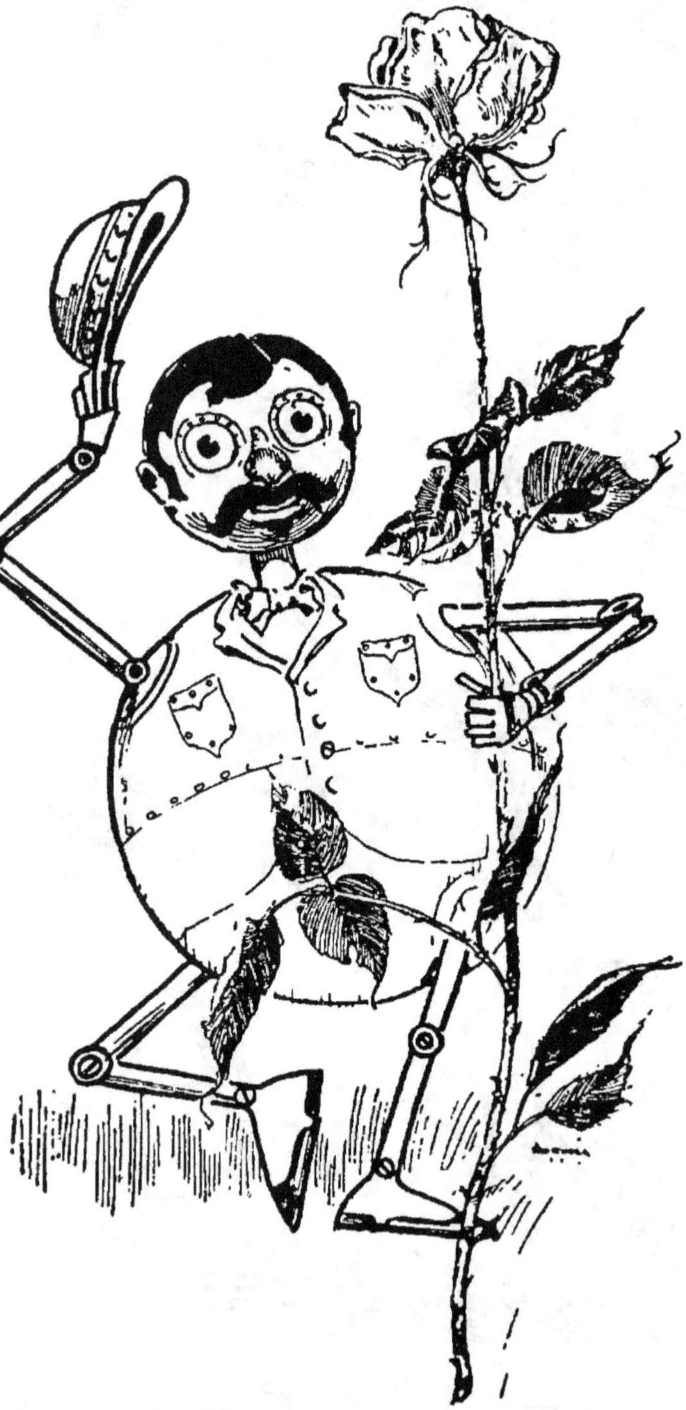

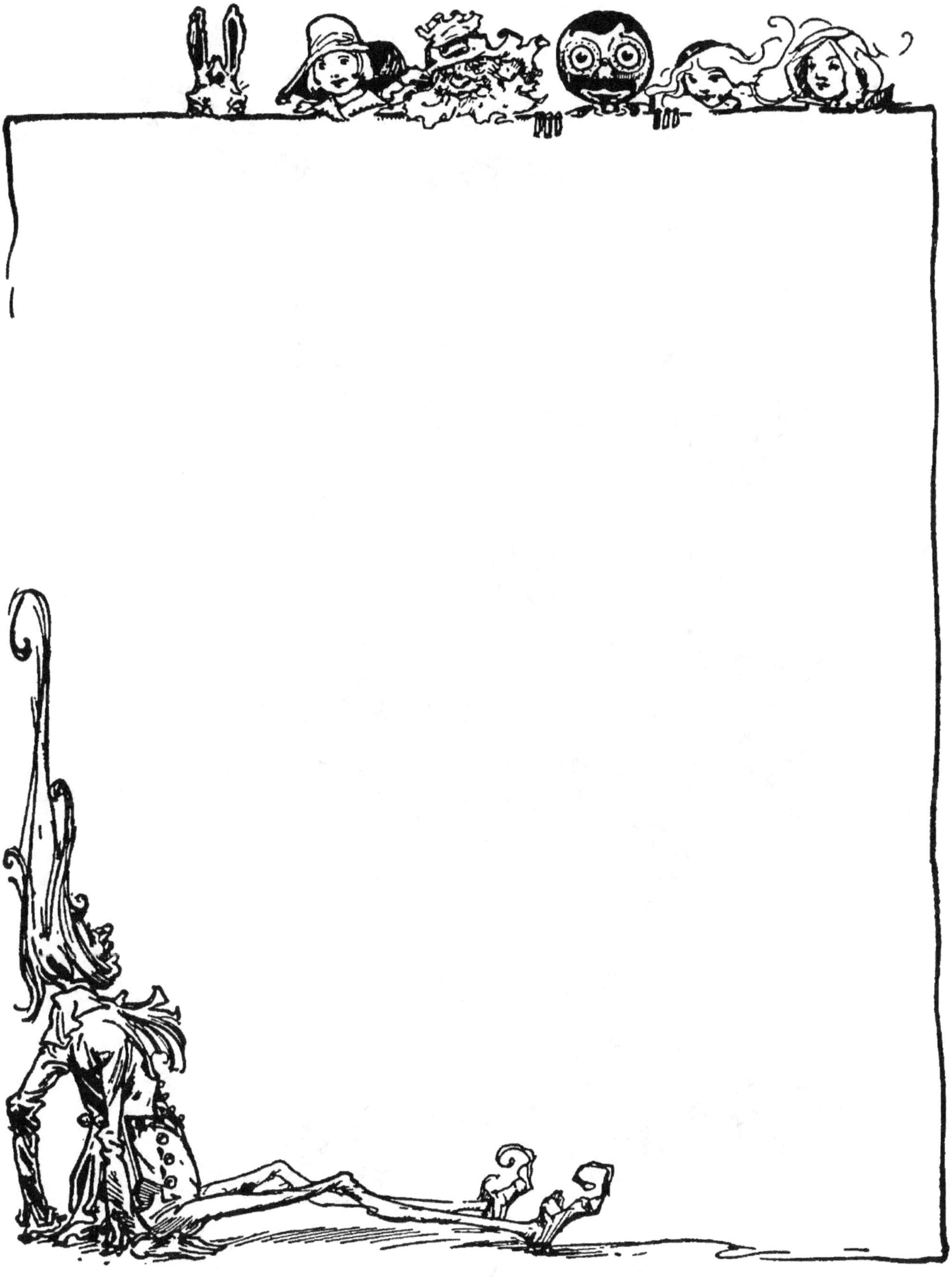

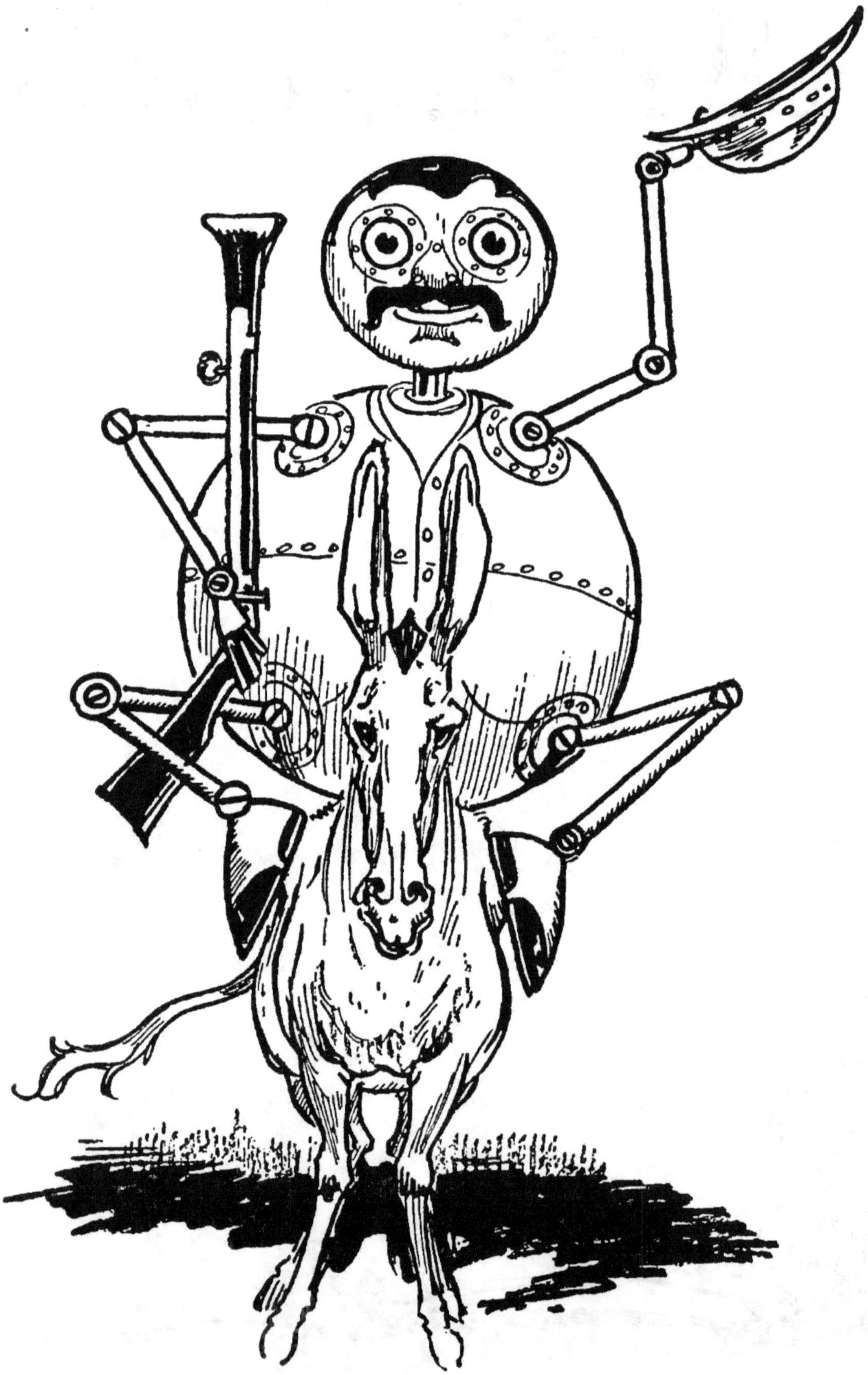

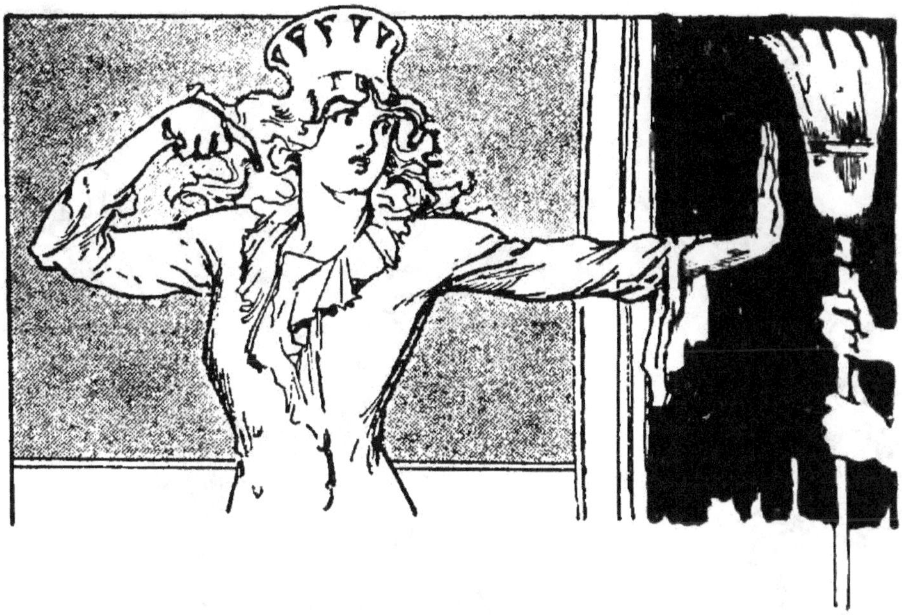

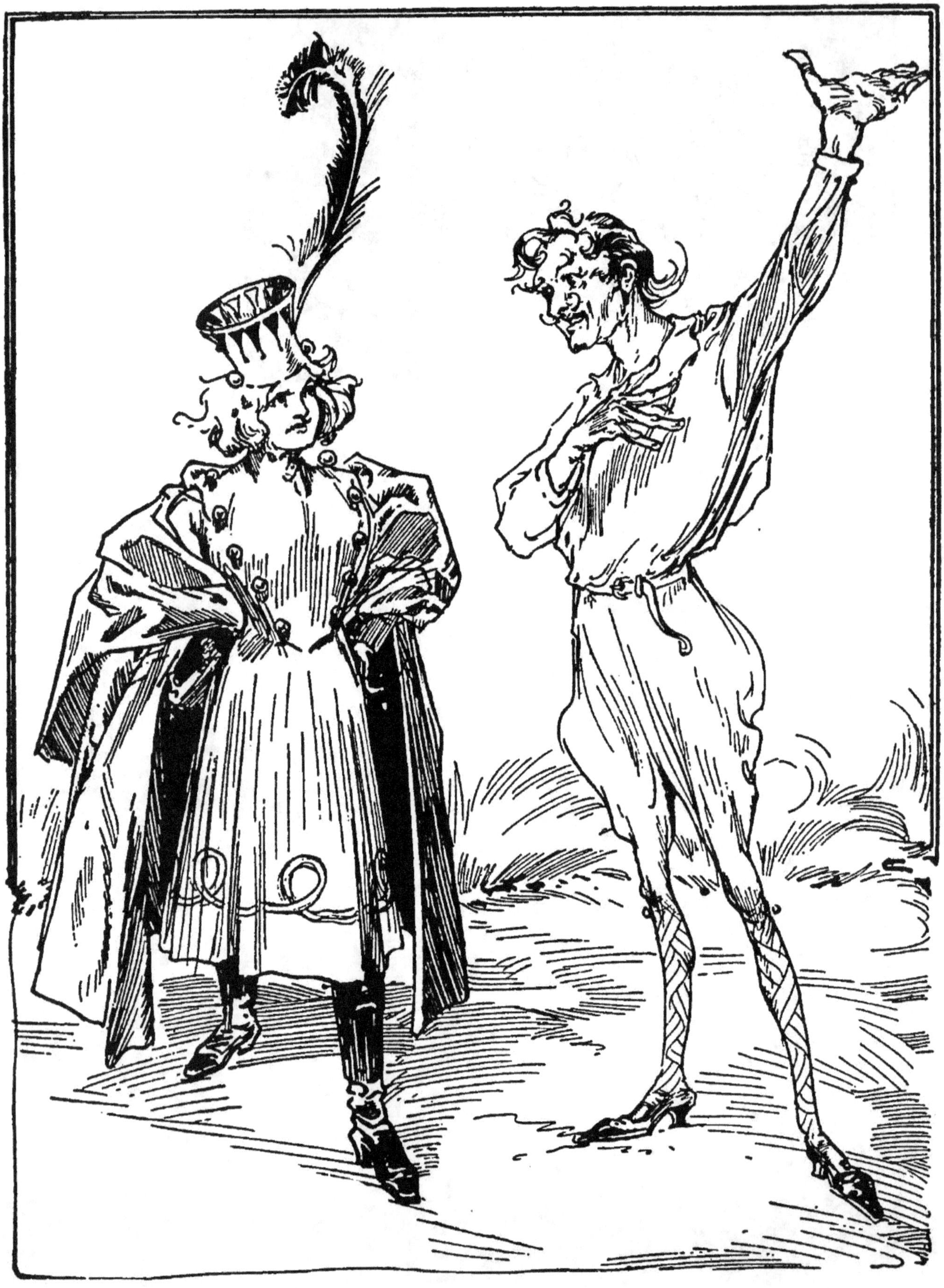

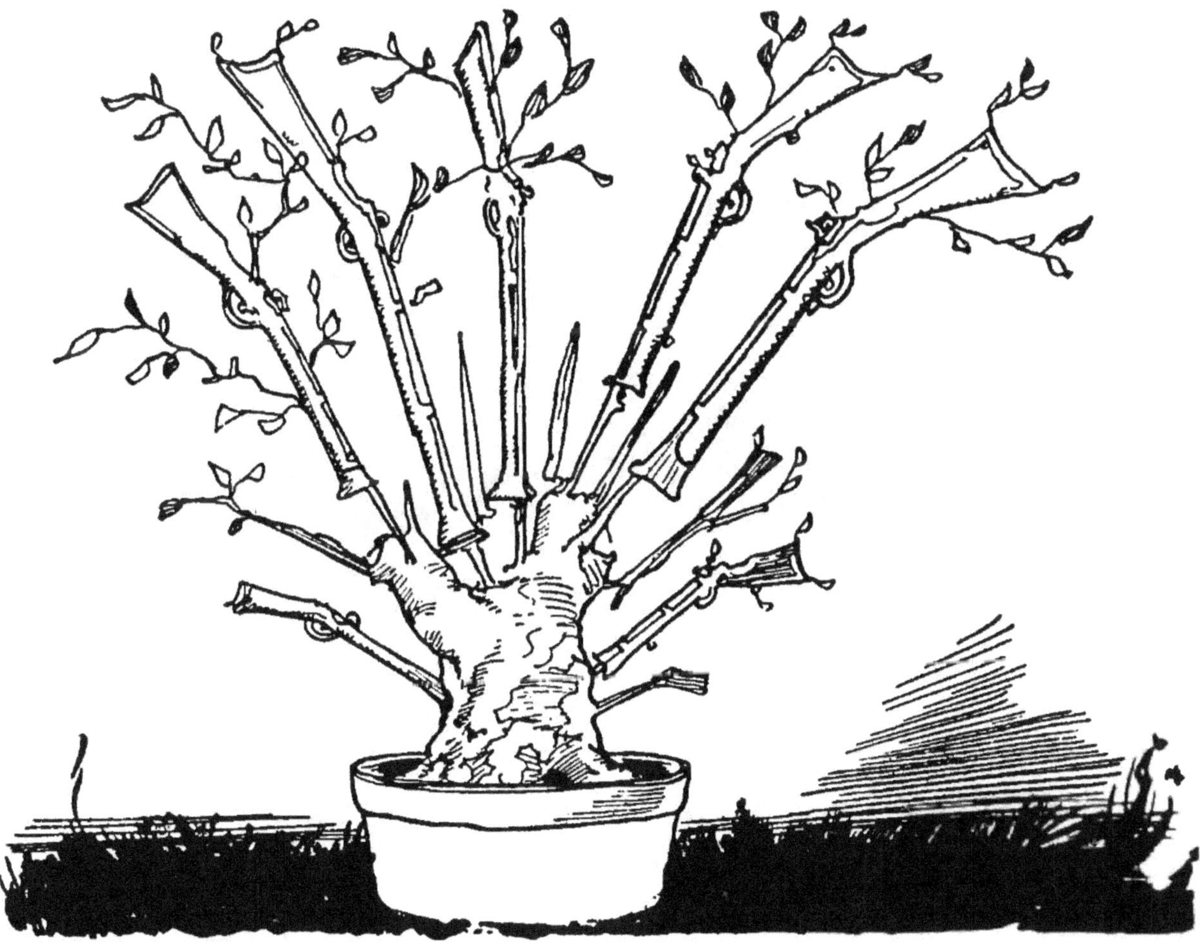

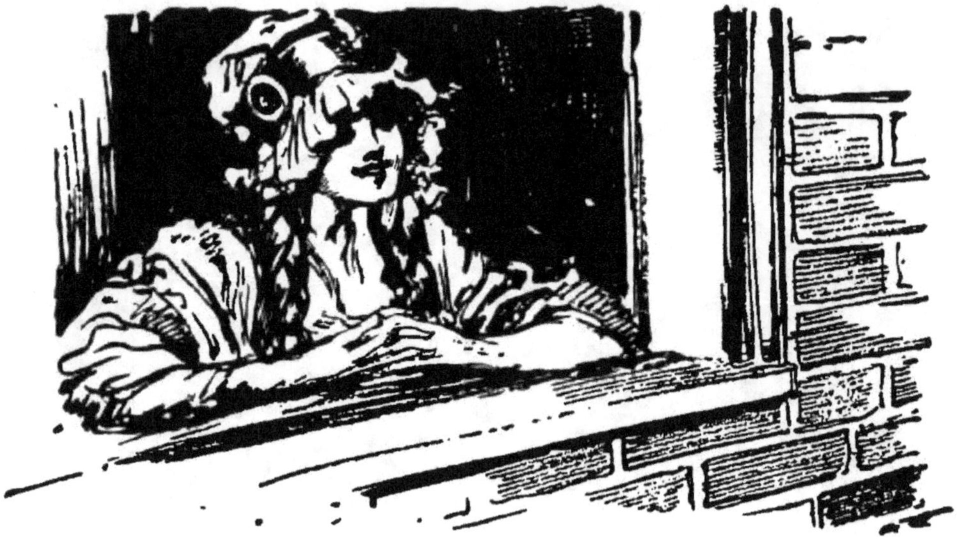

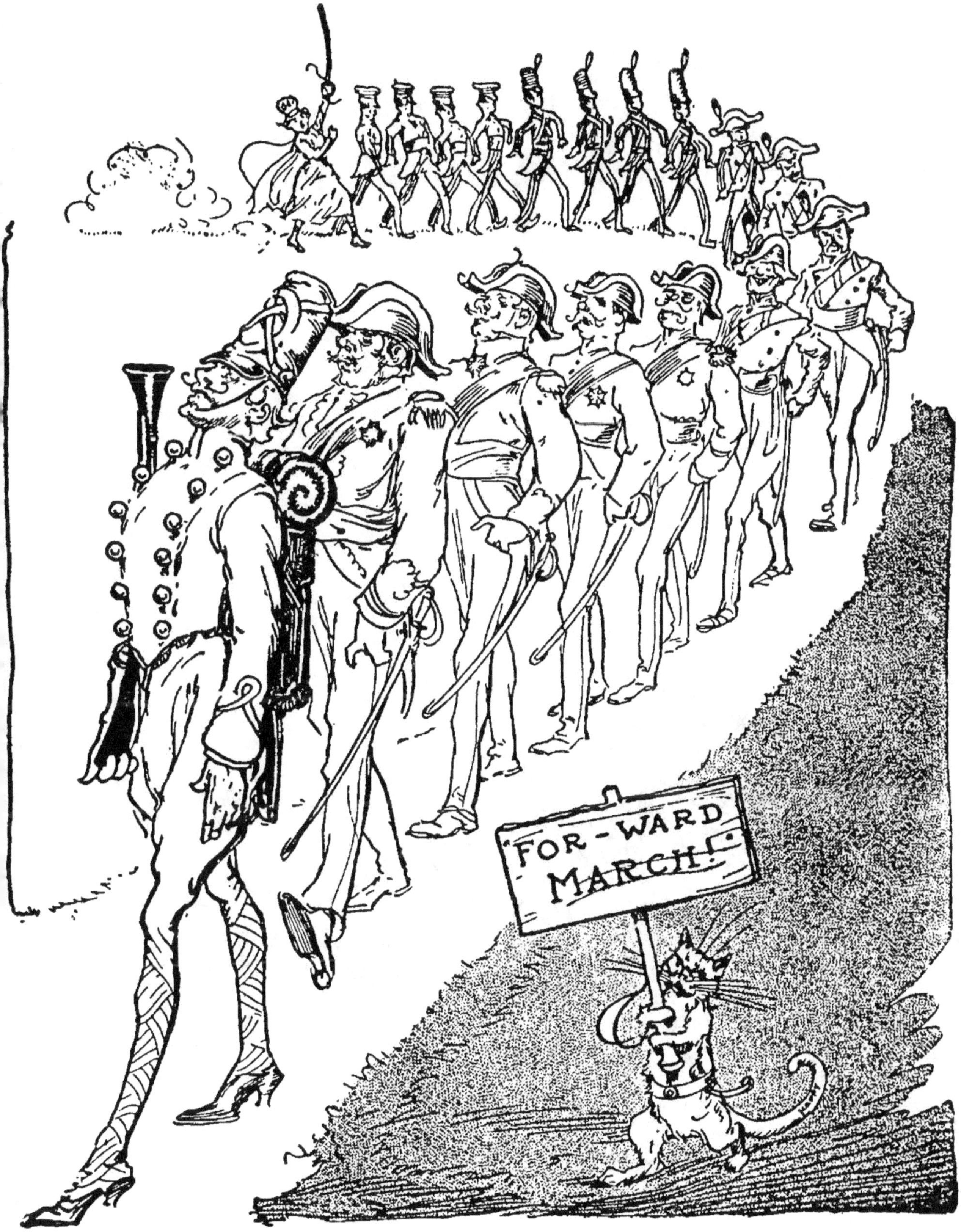
FOR-WARD
MARCH!

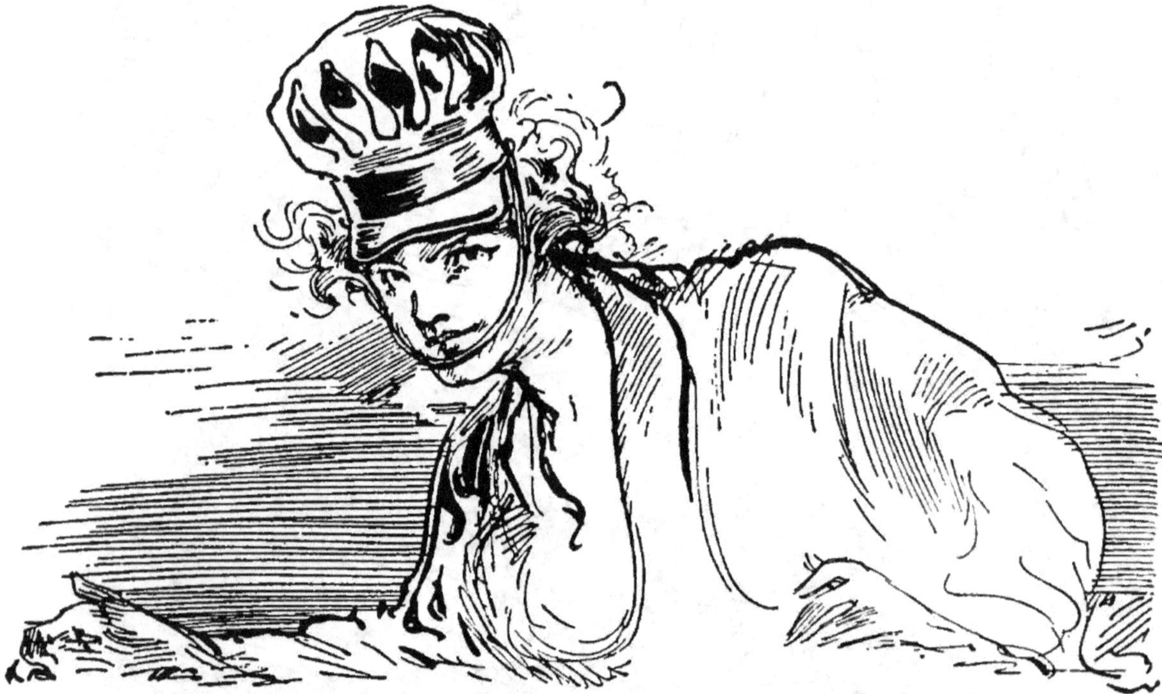

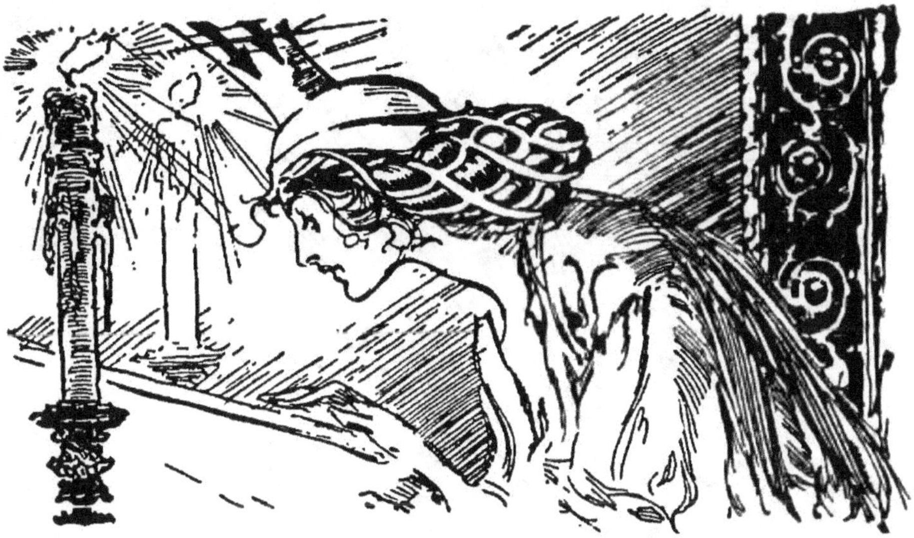

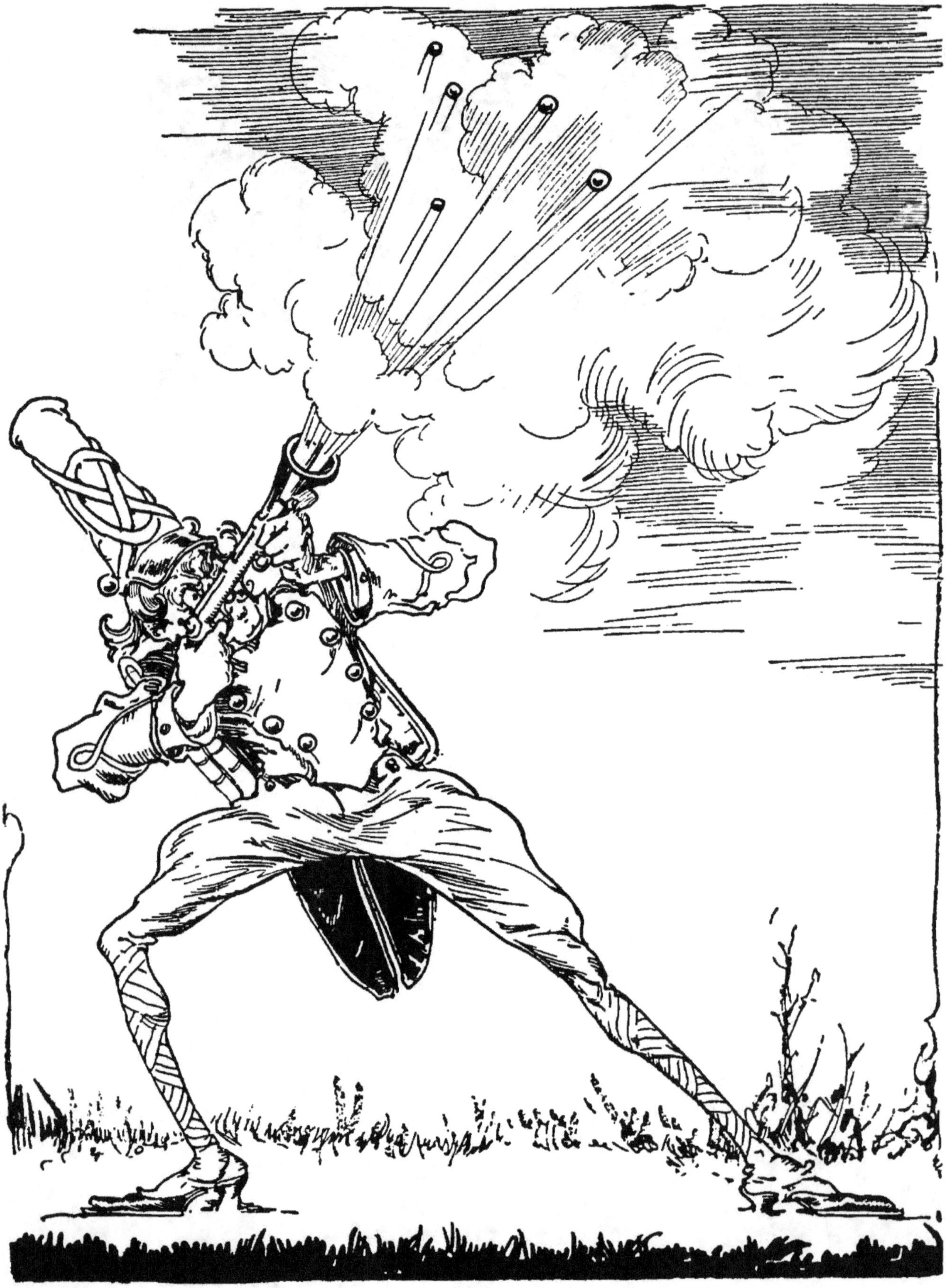

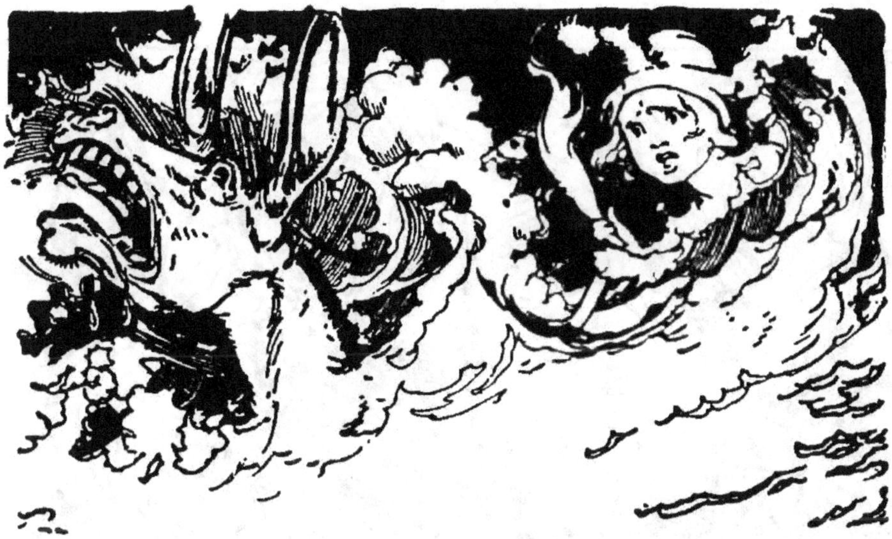

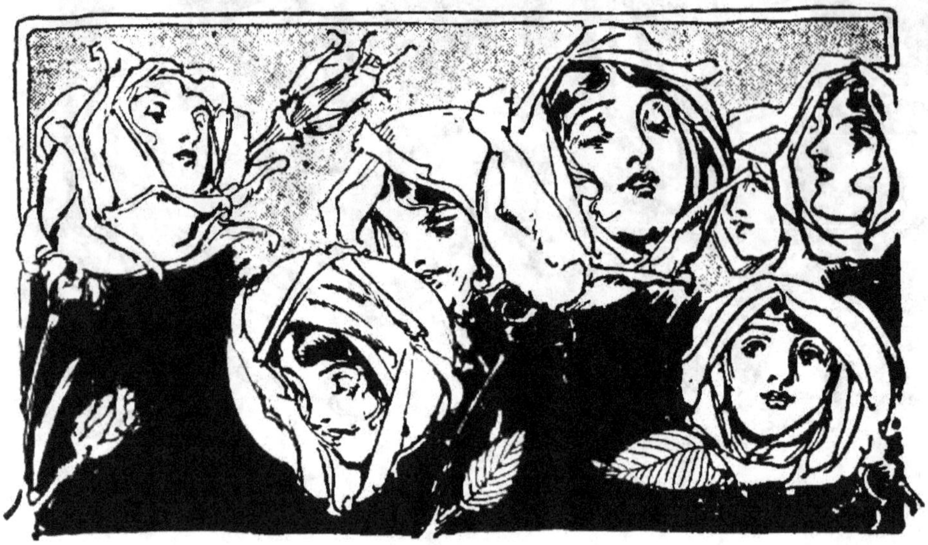

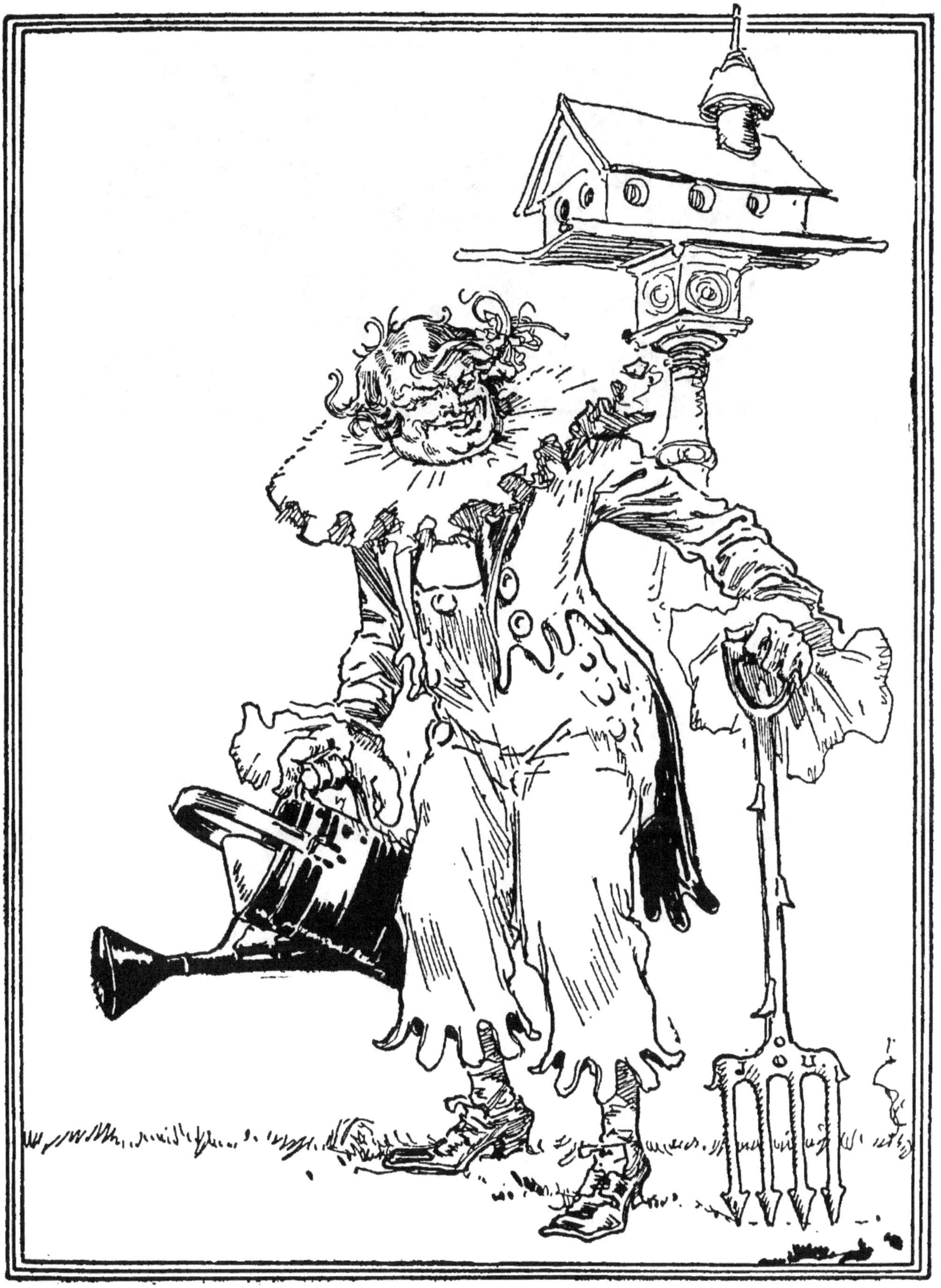

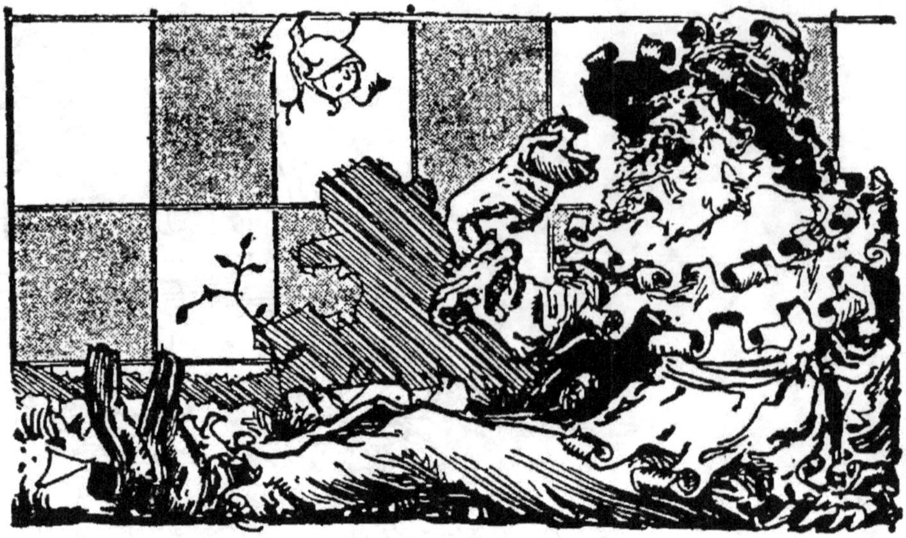

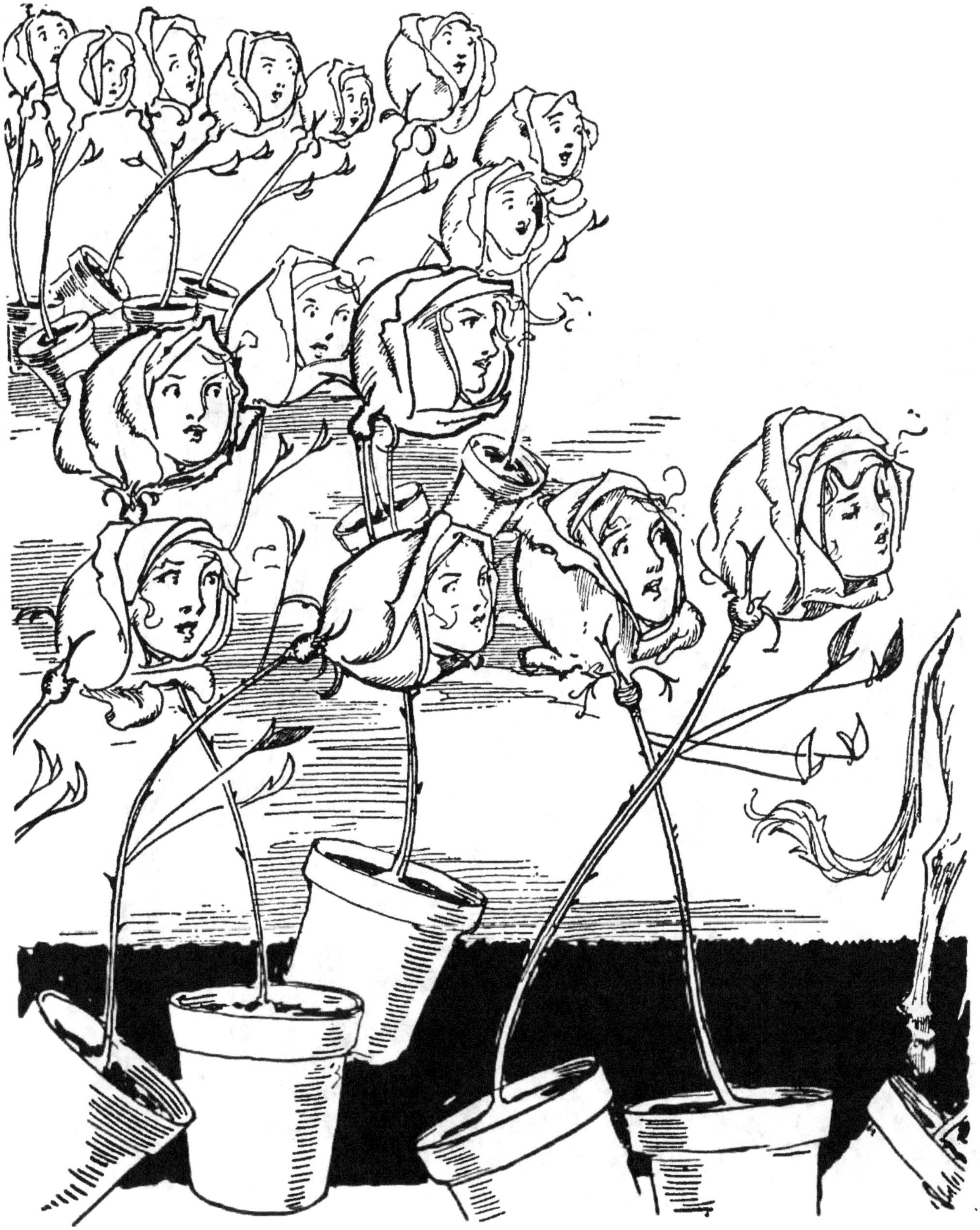

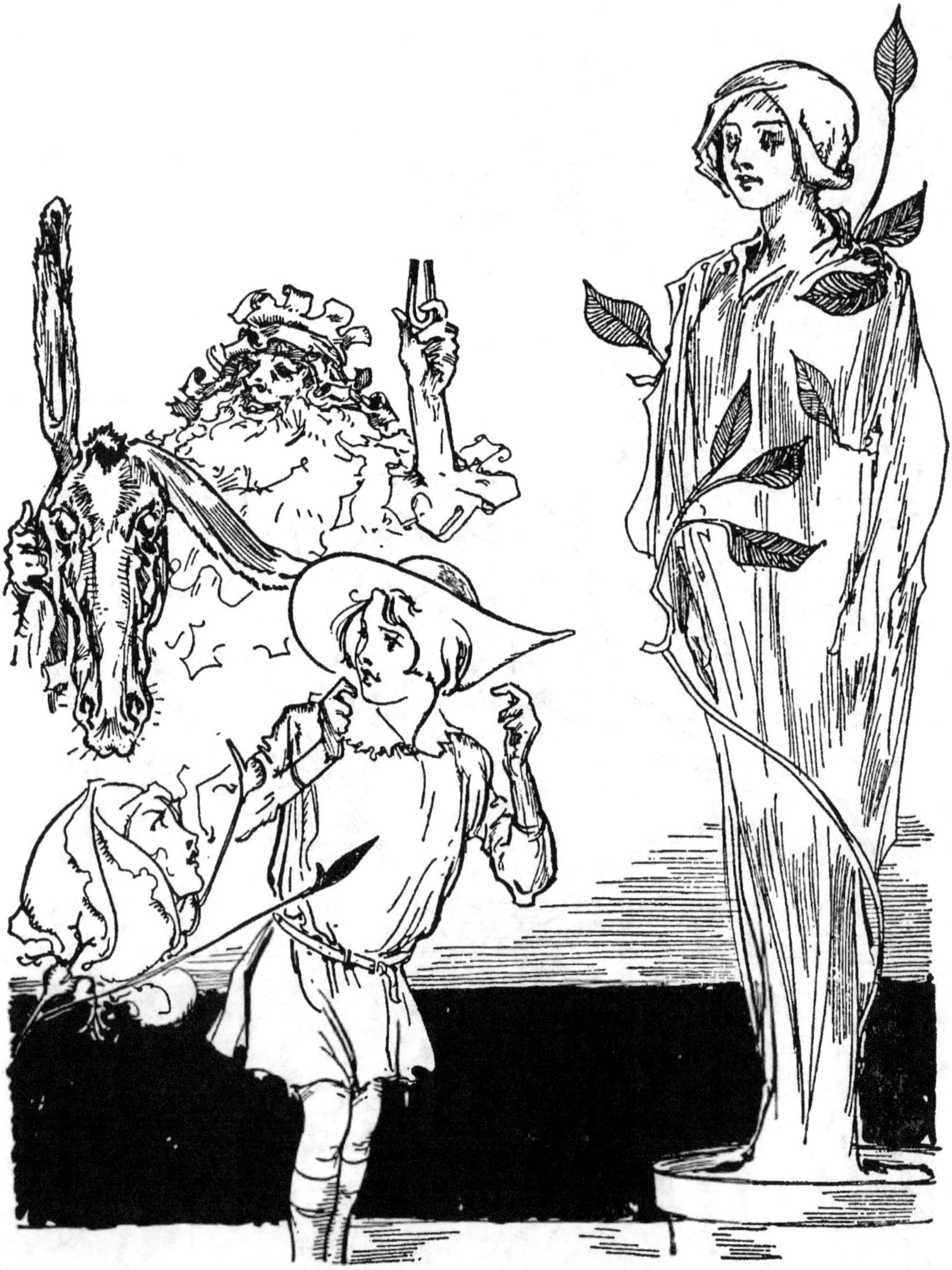

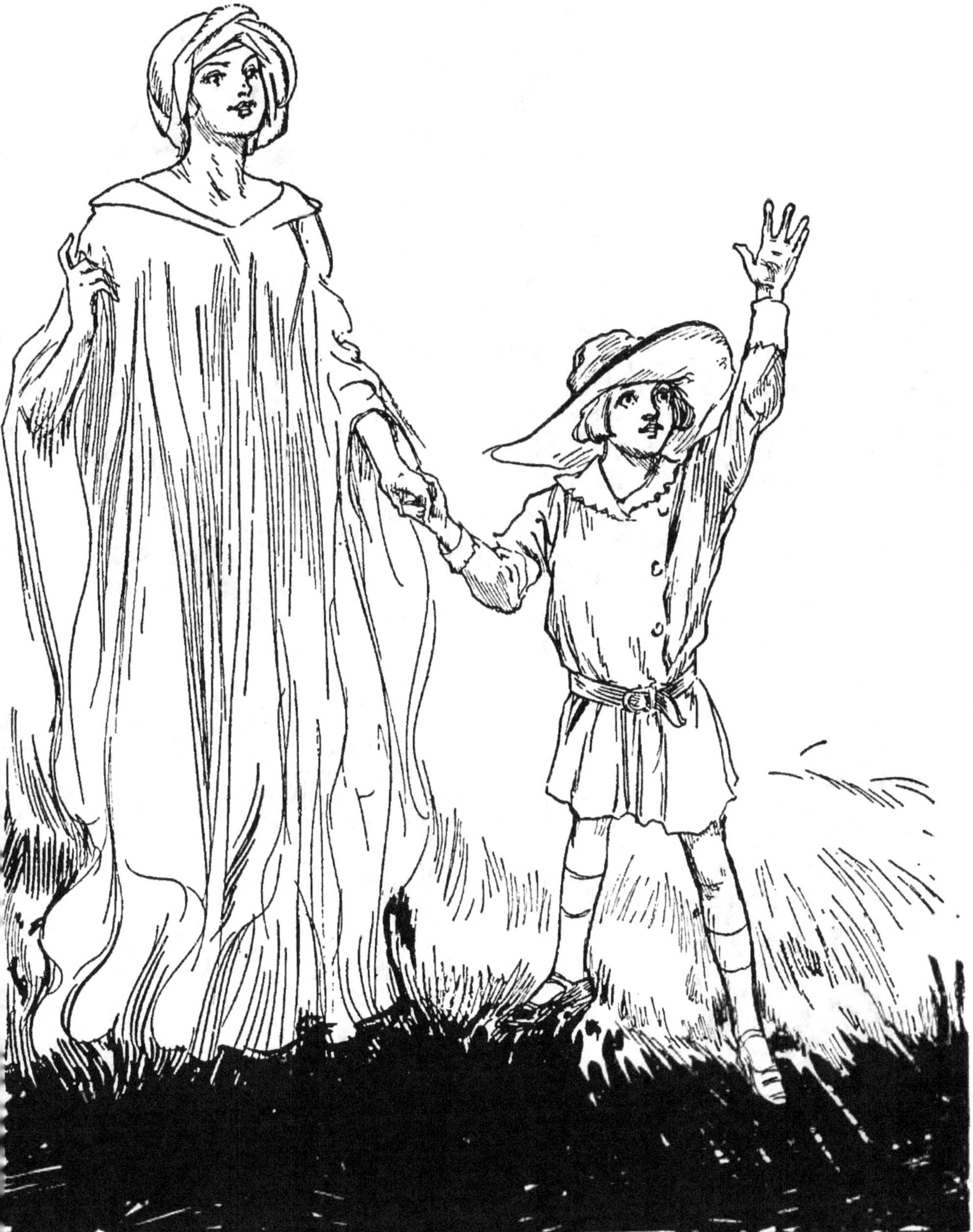

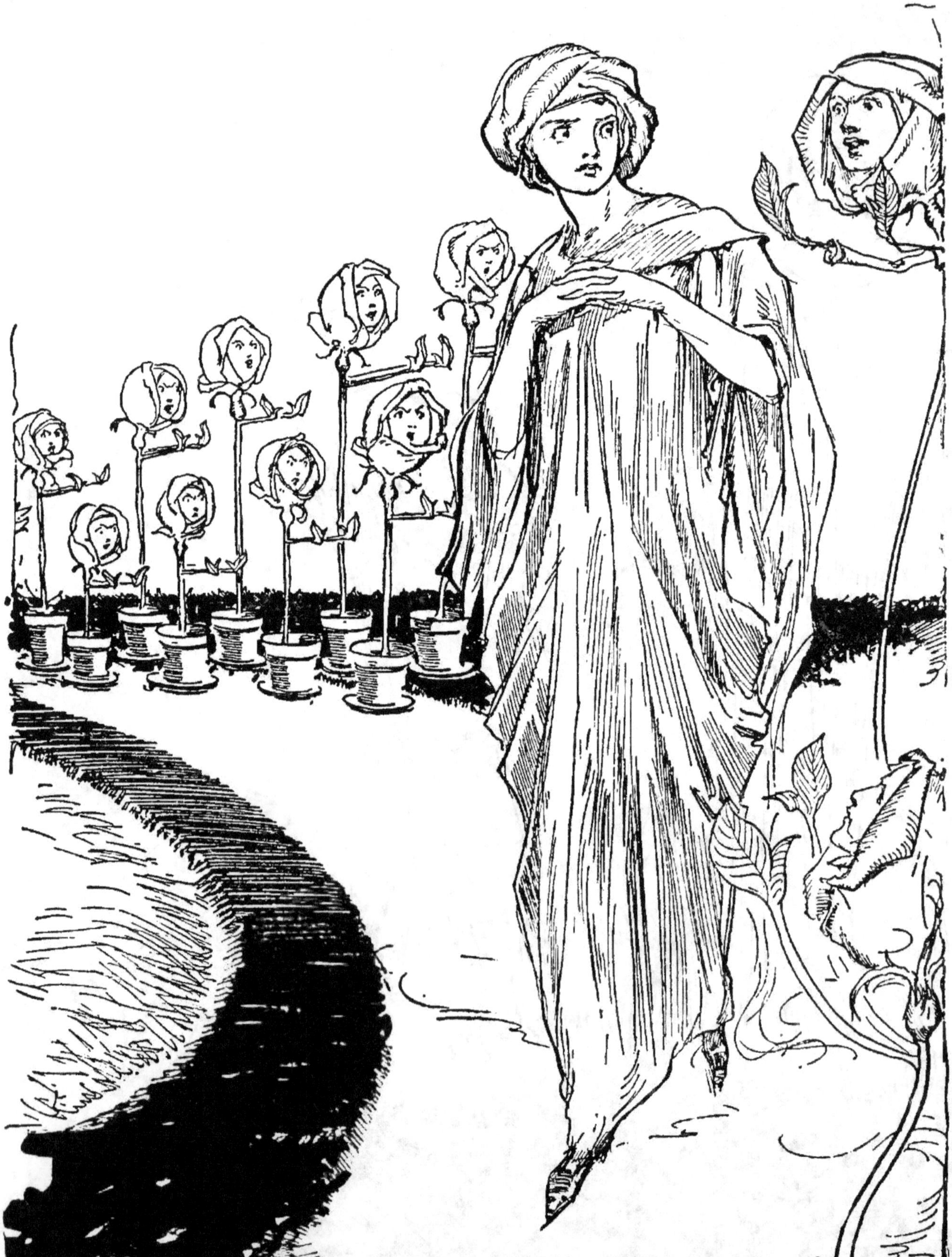

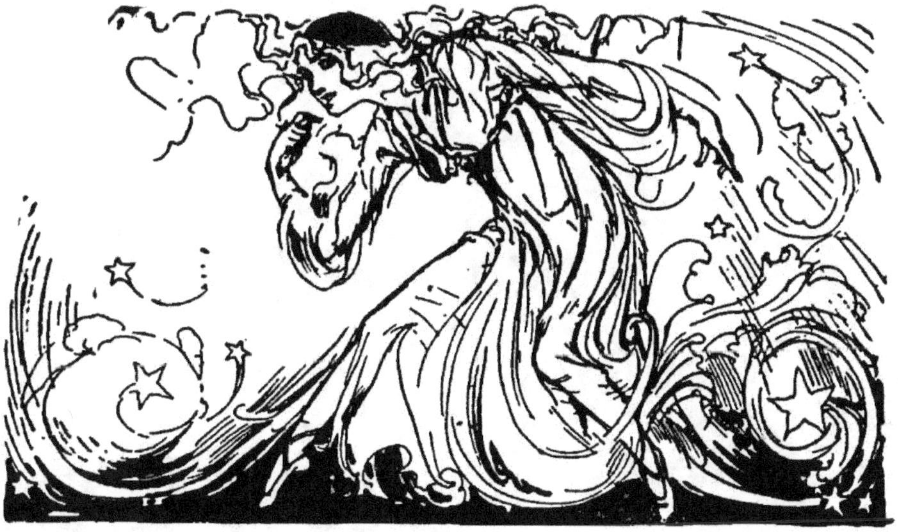

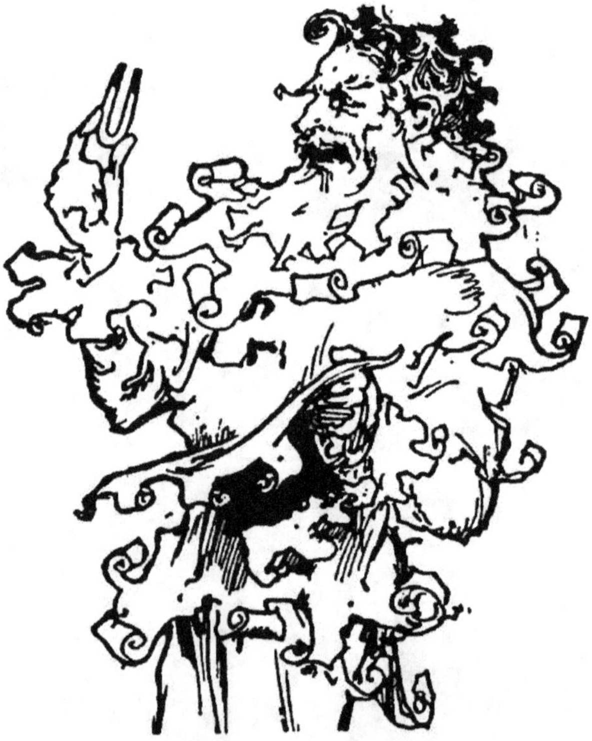

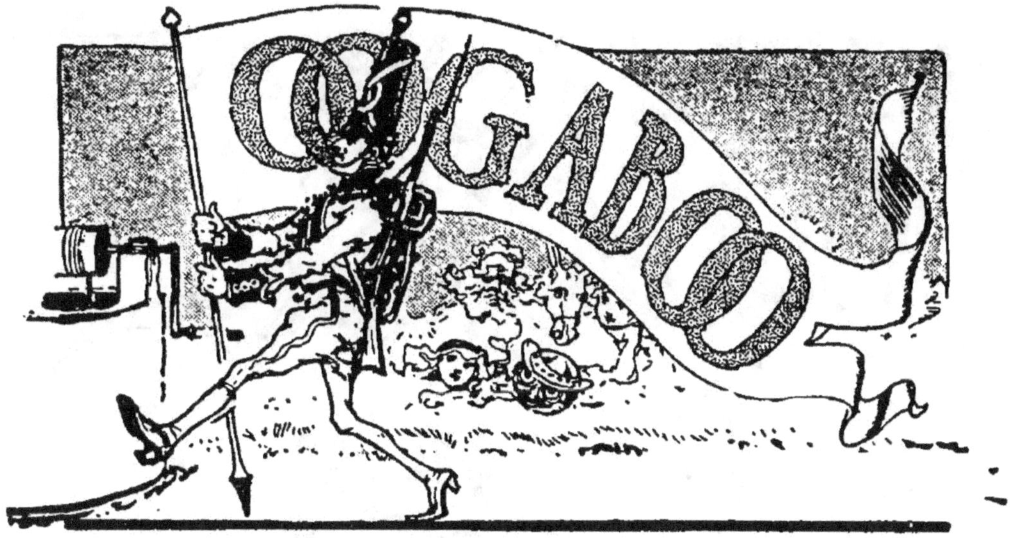
OOGABOOS

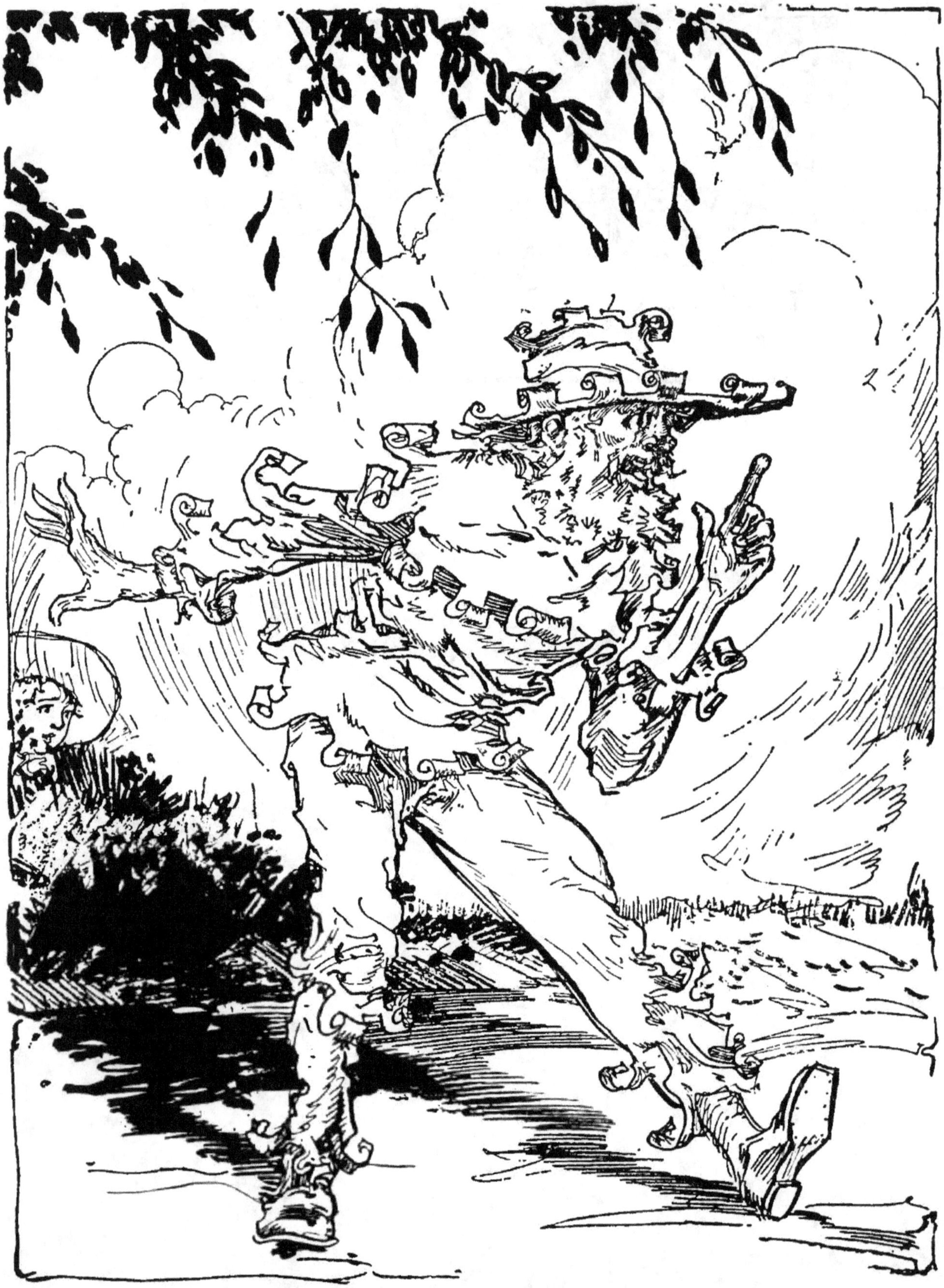

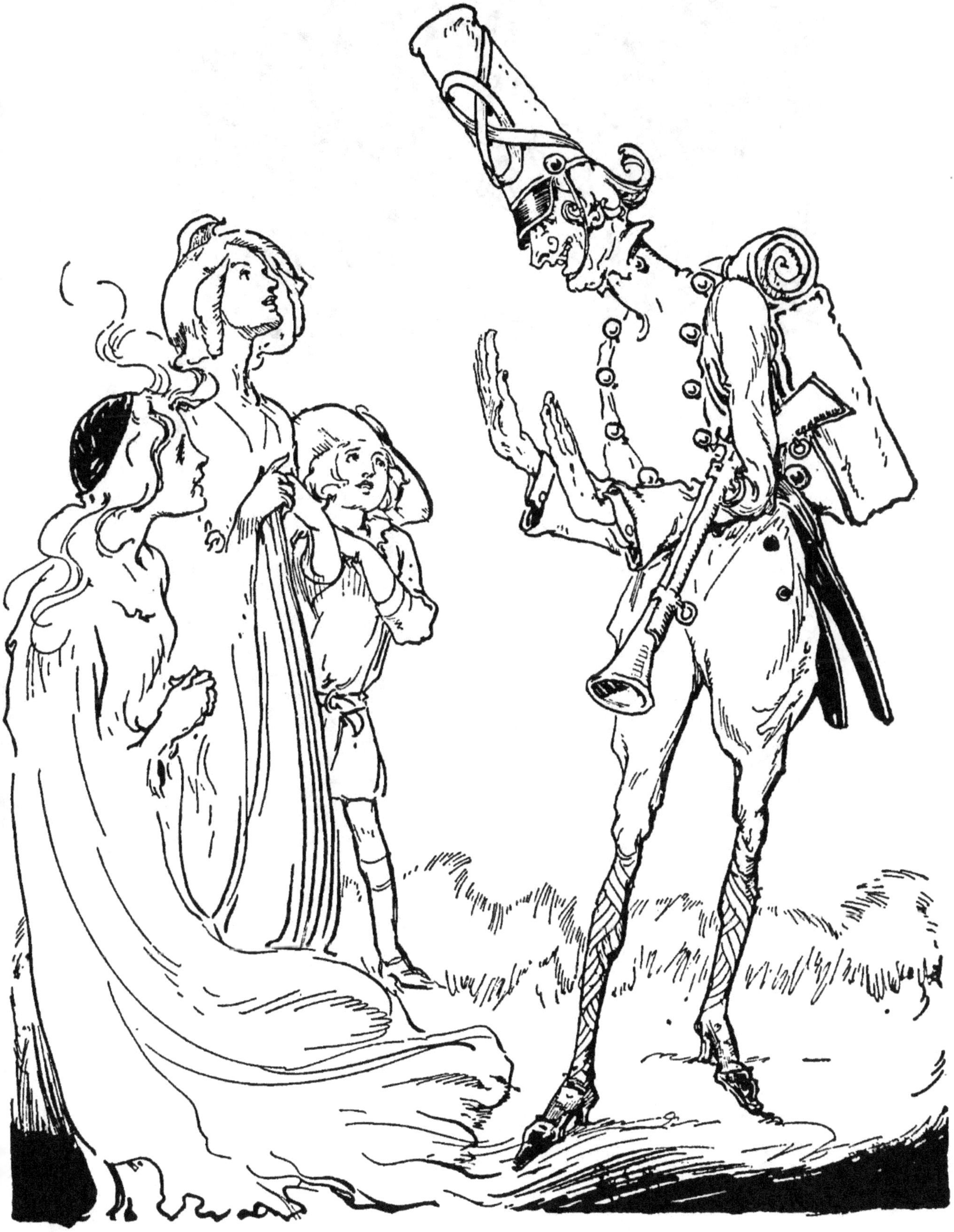

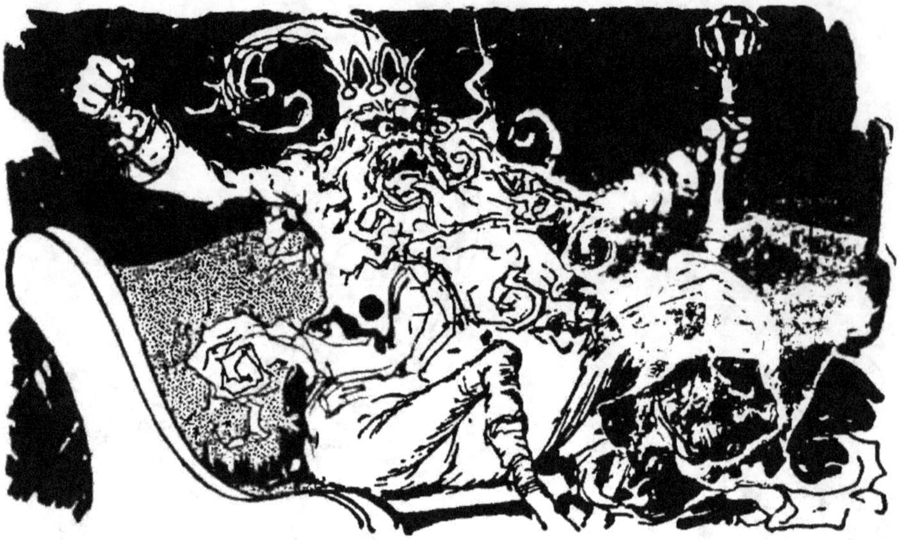

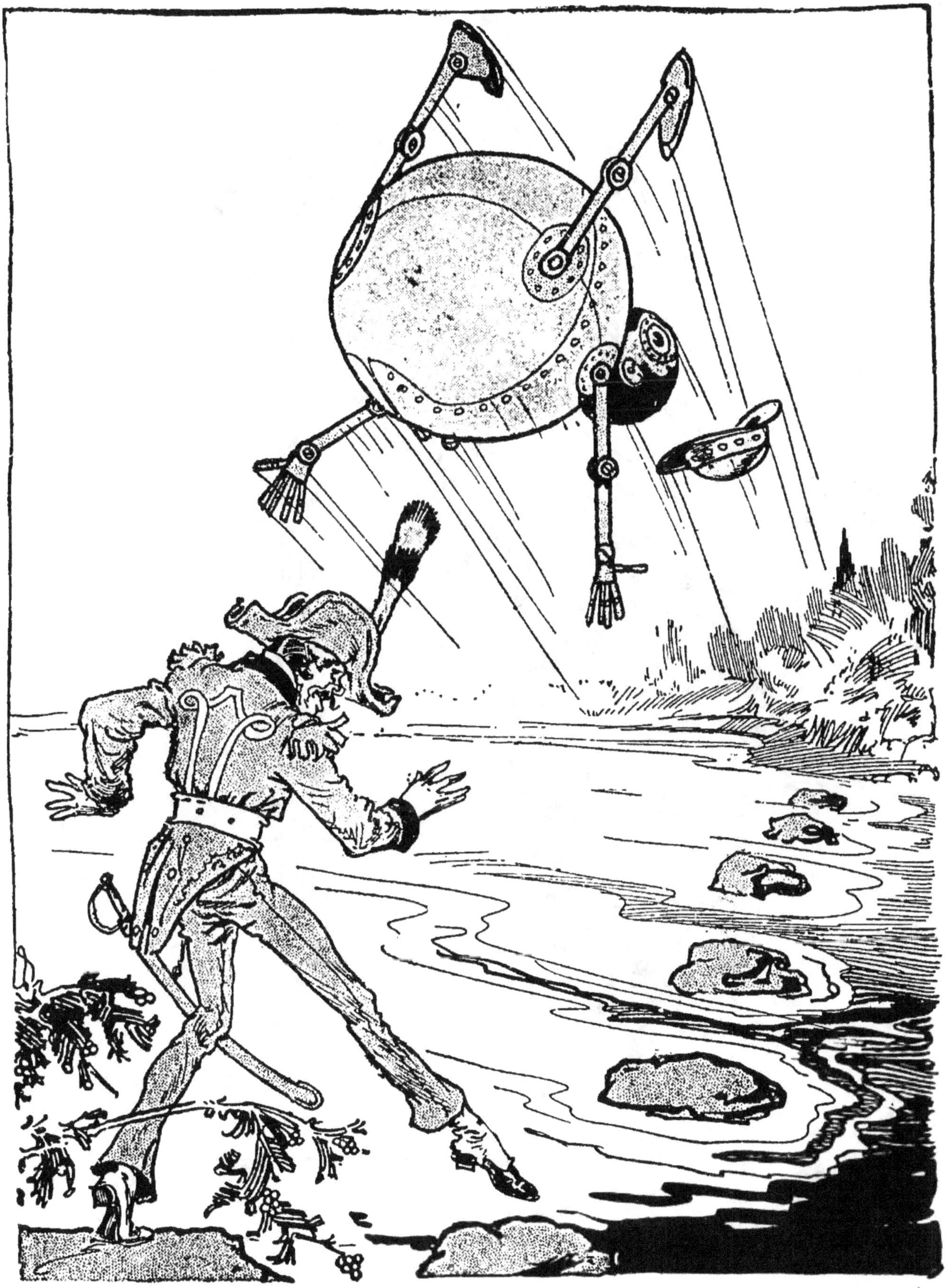

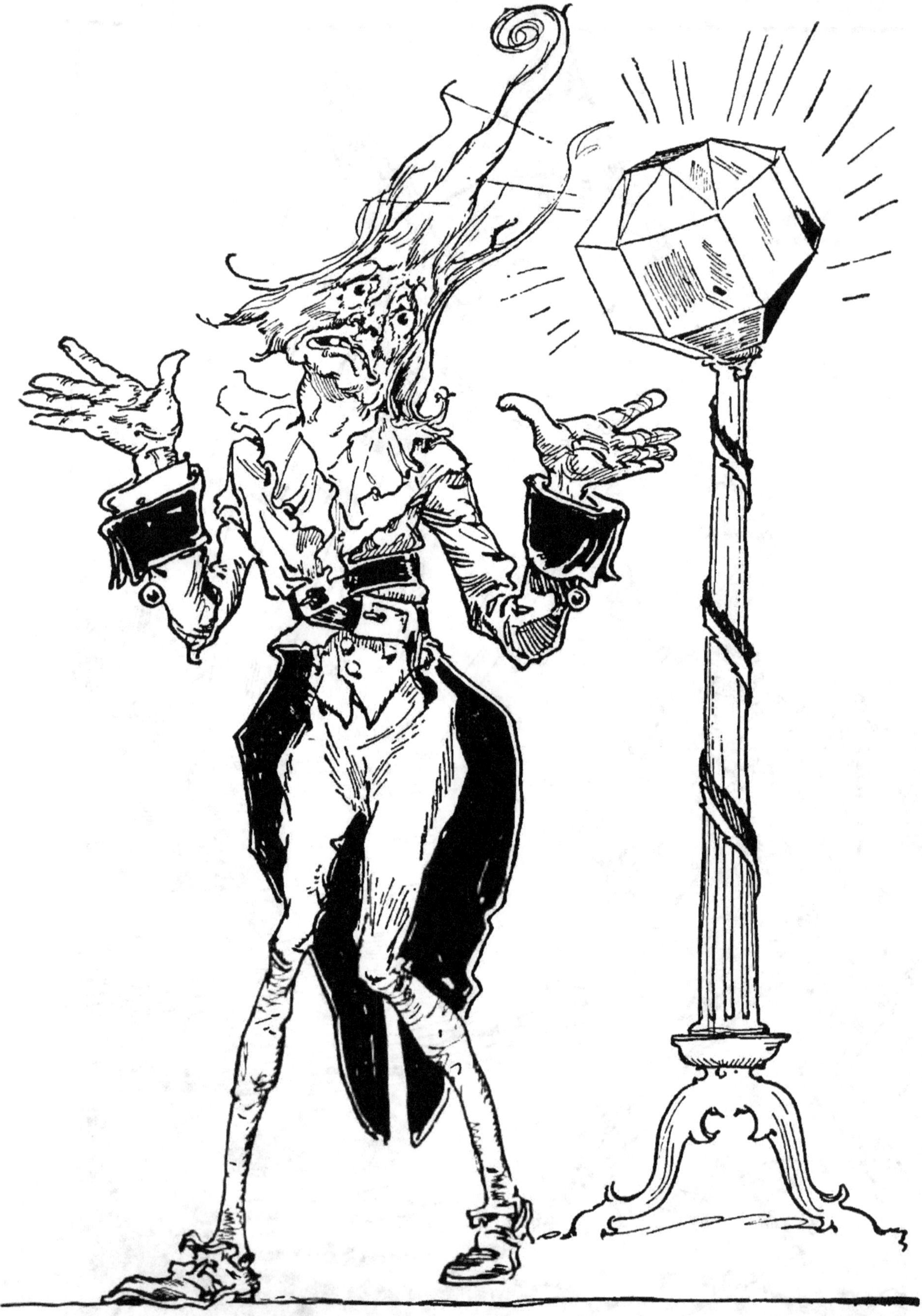

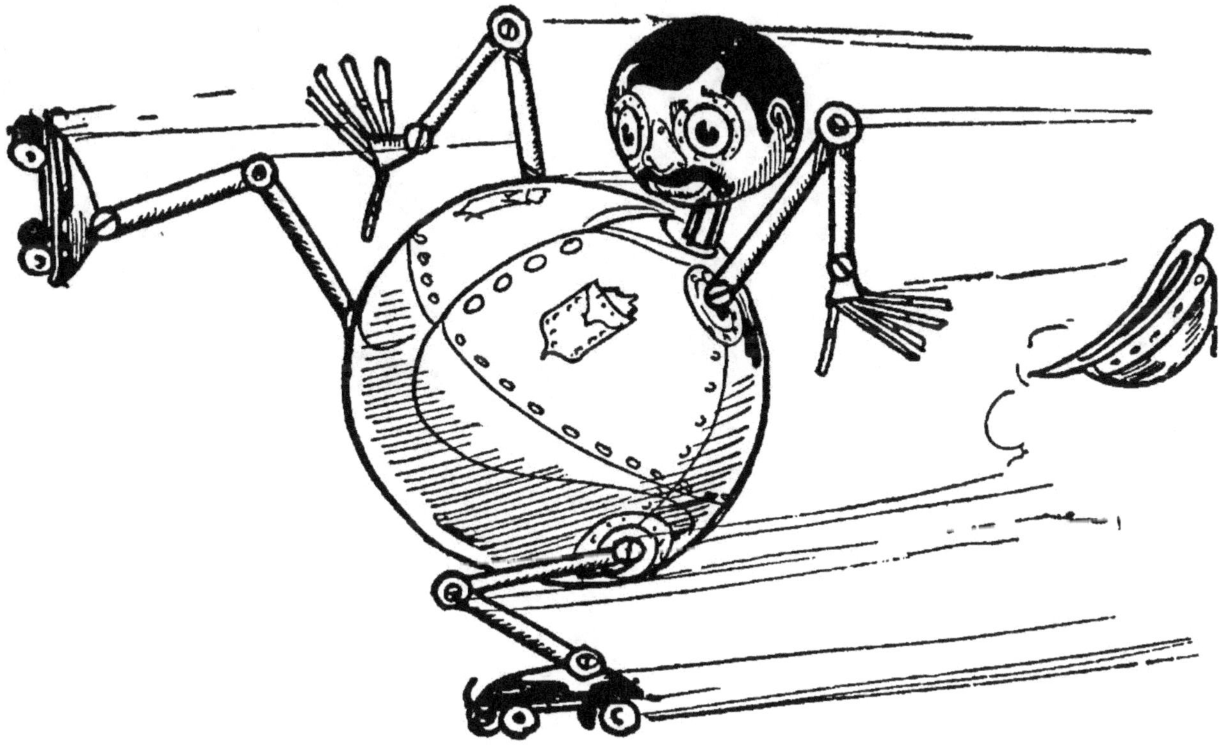

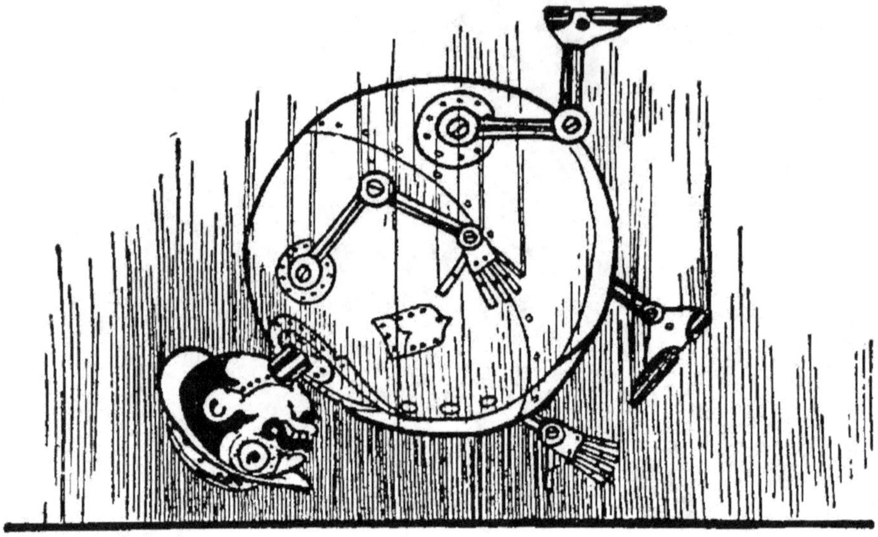

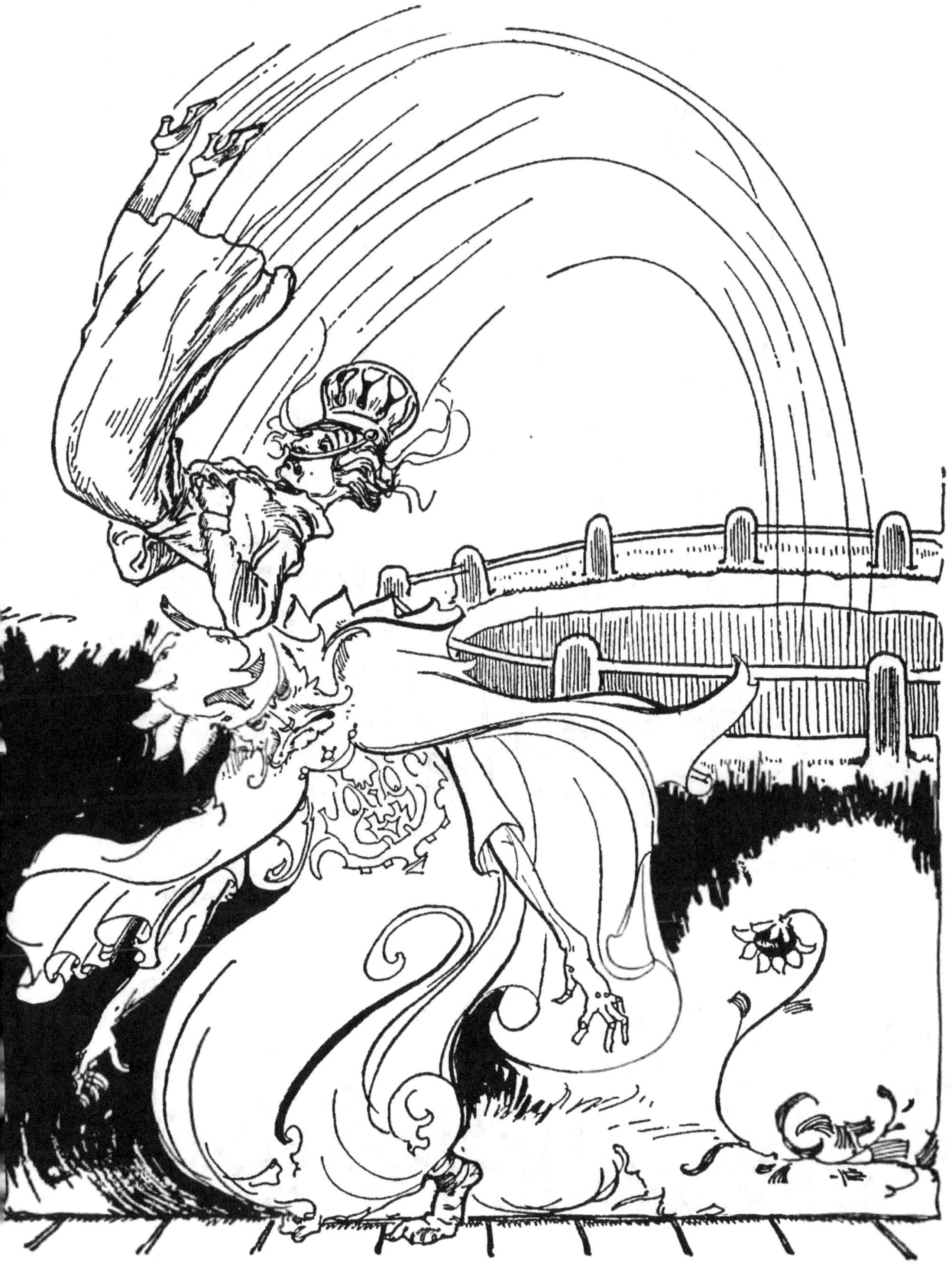

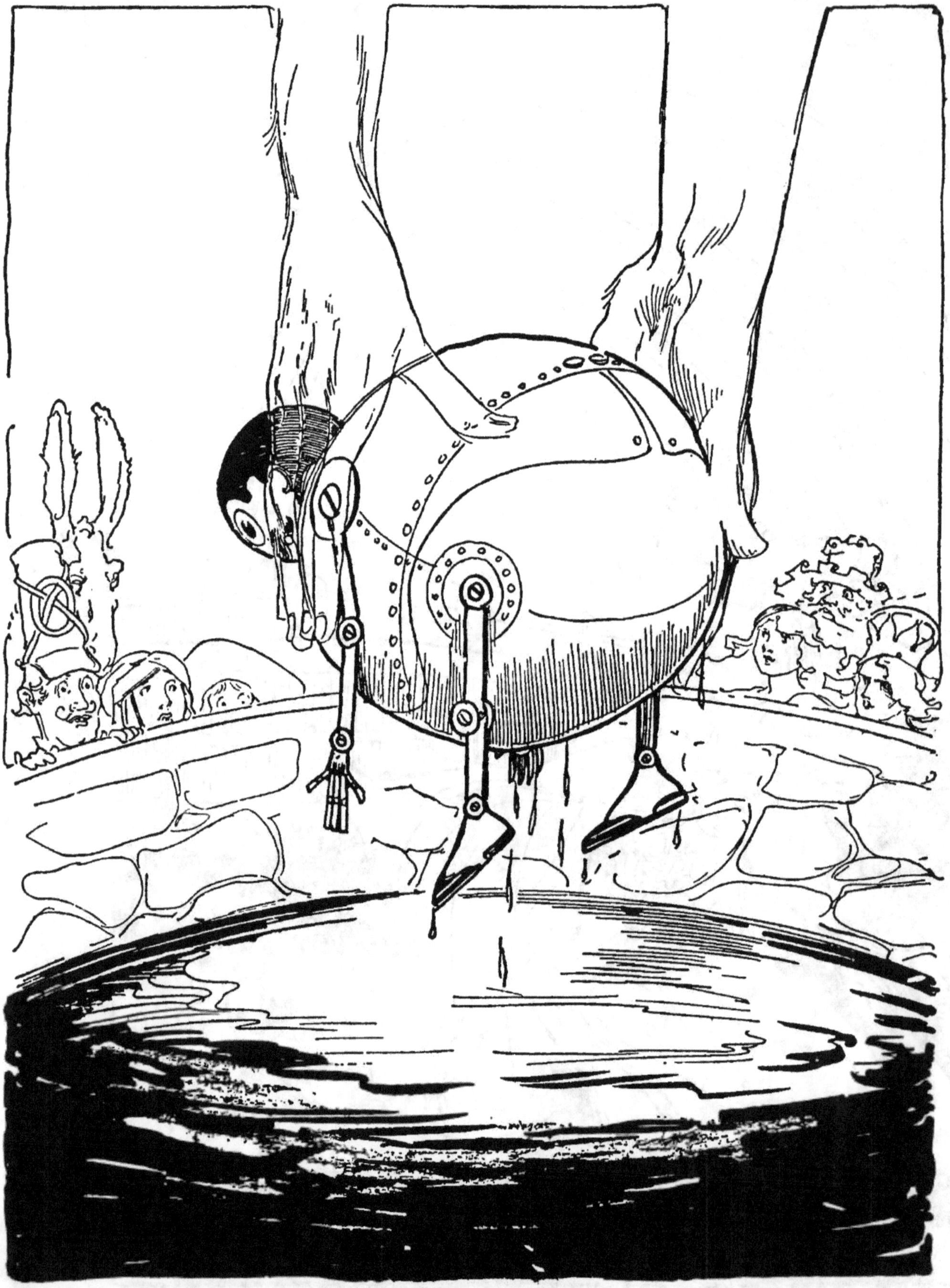

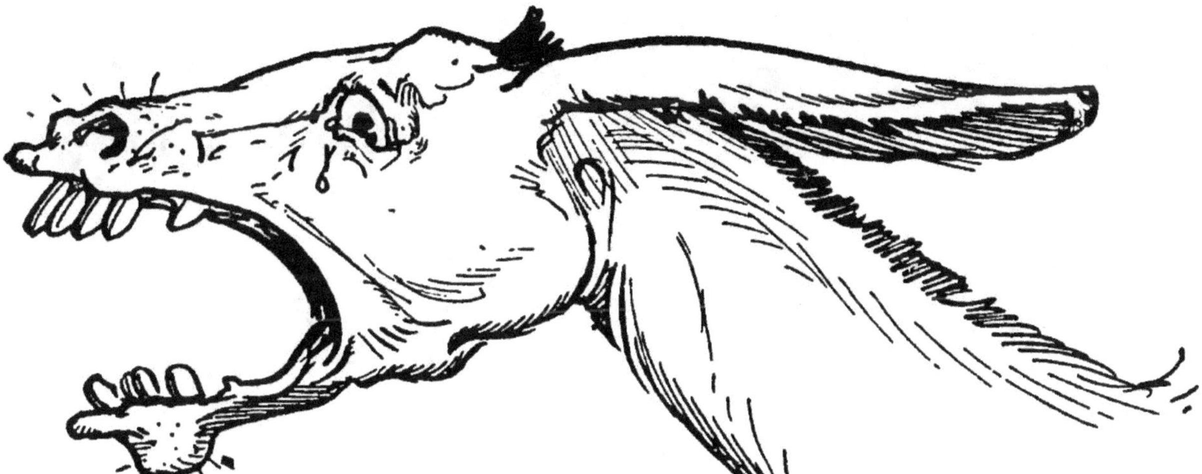

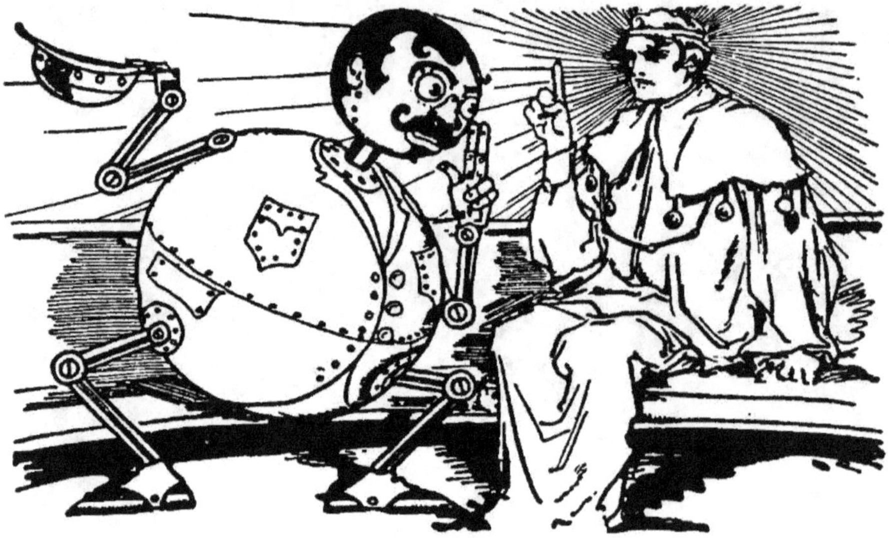

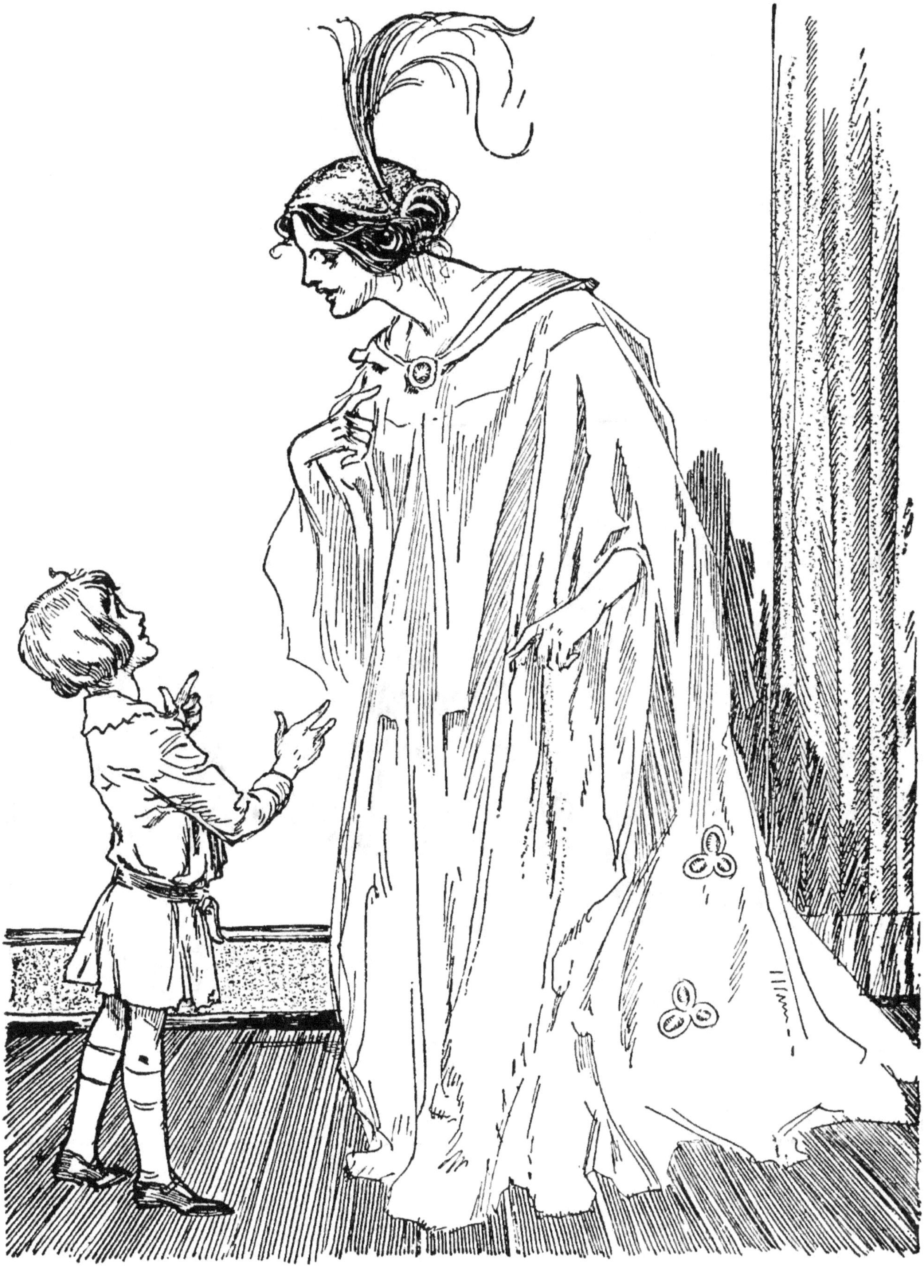

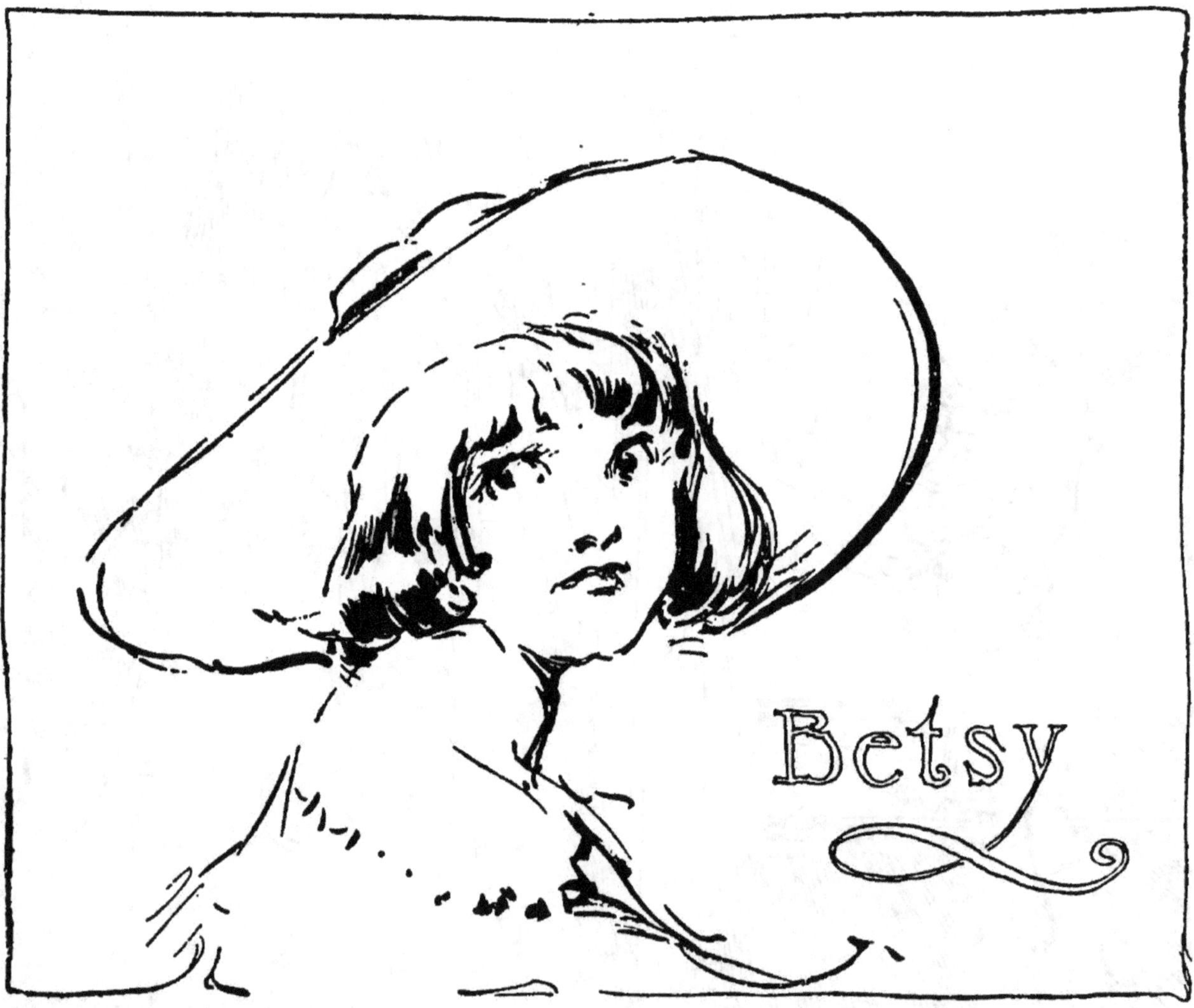
Betsy

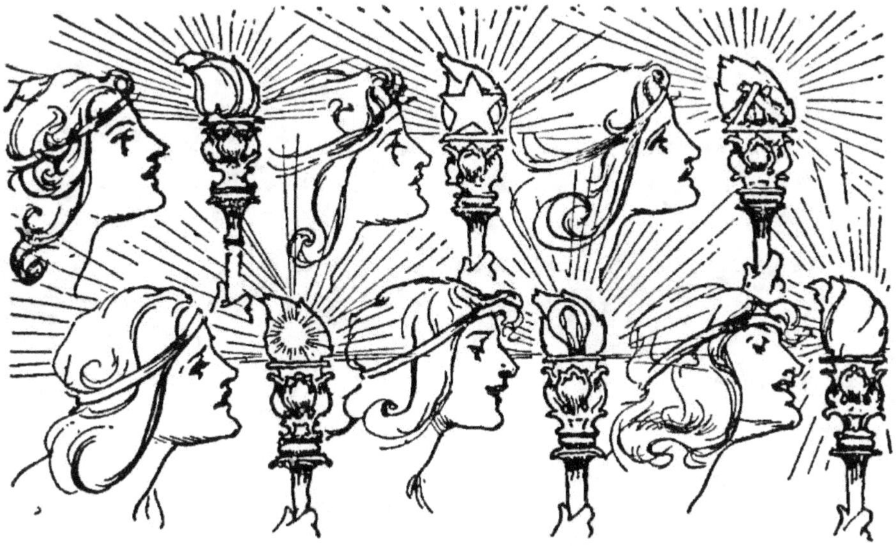

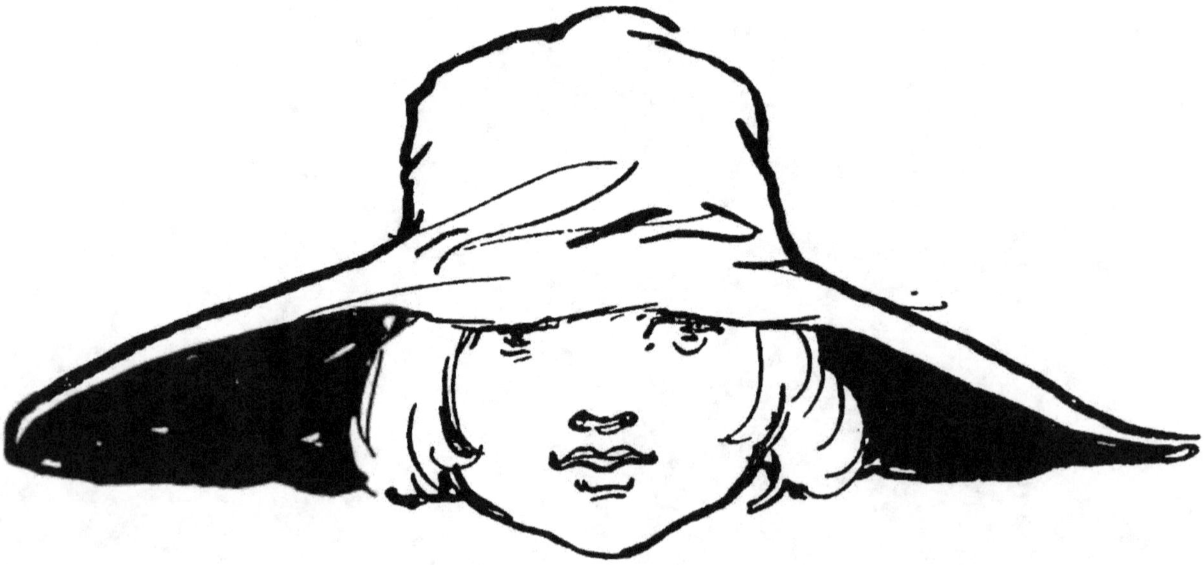

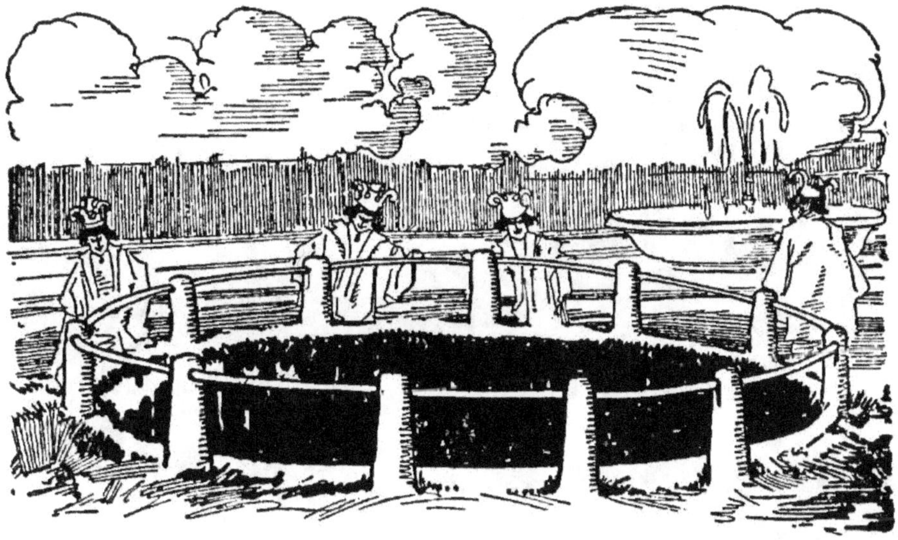

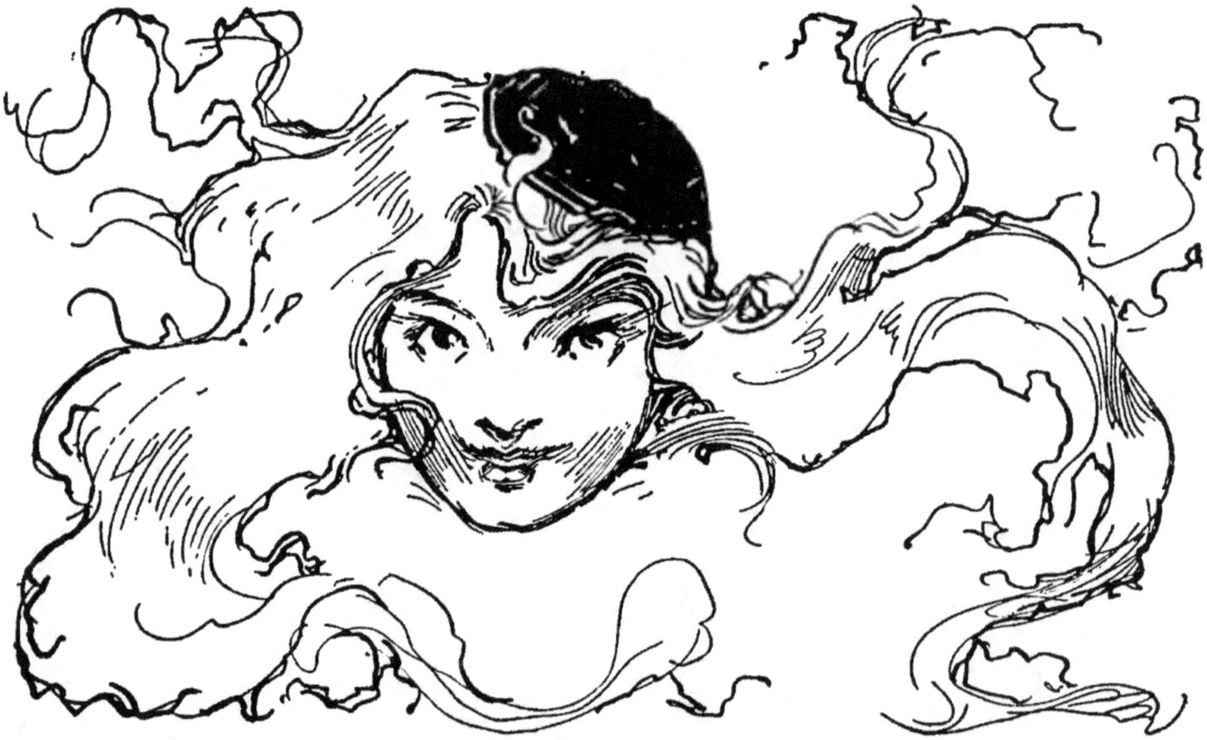

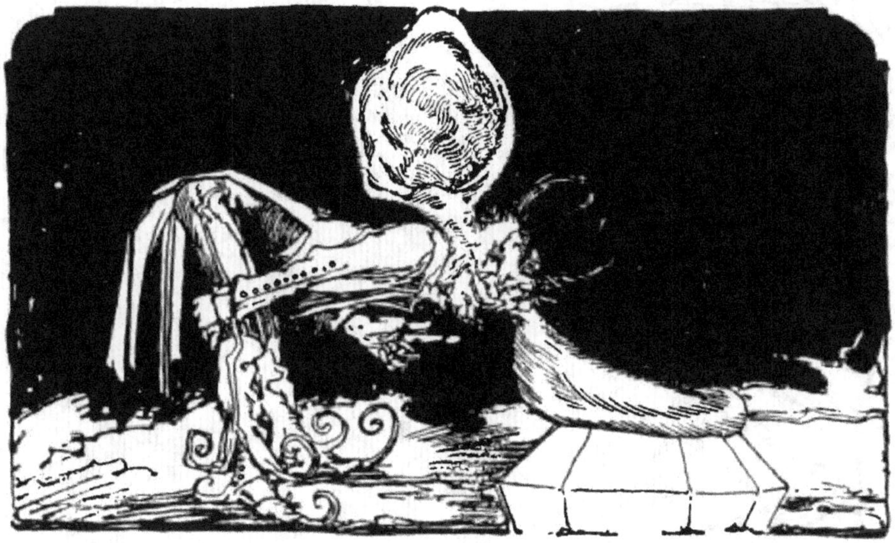

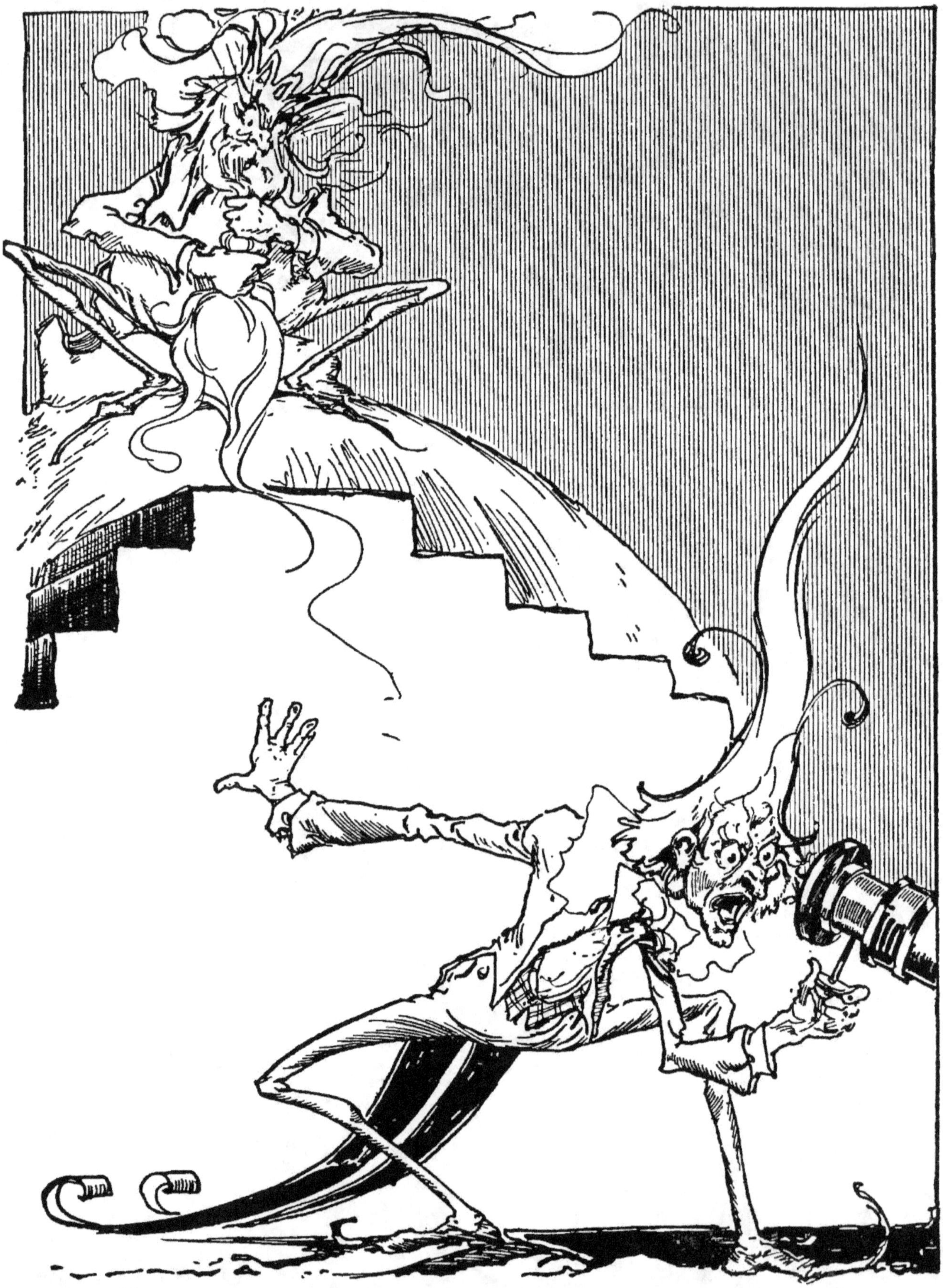

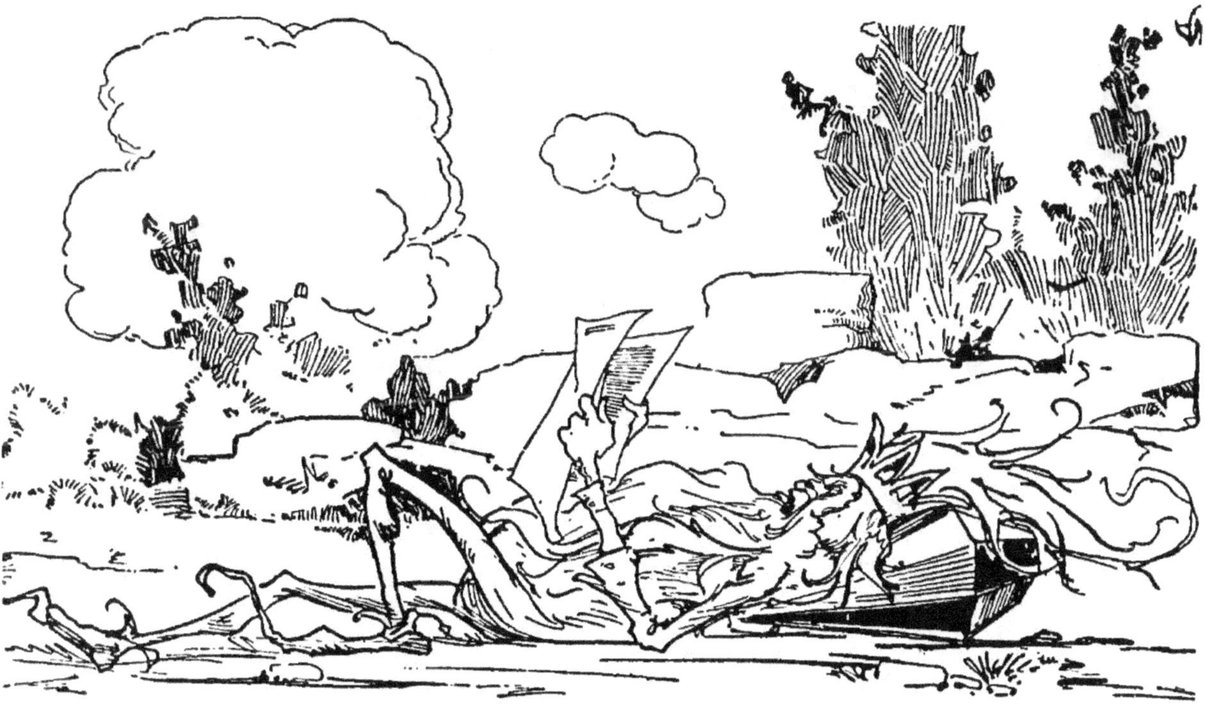

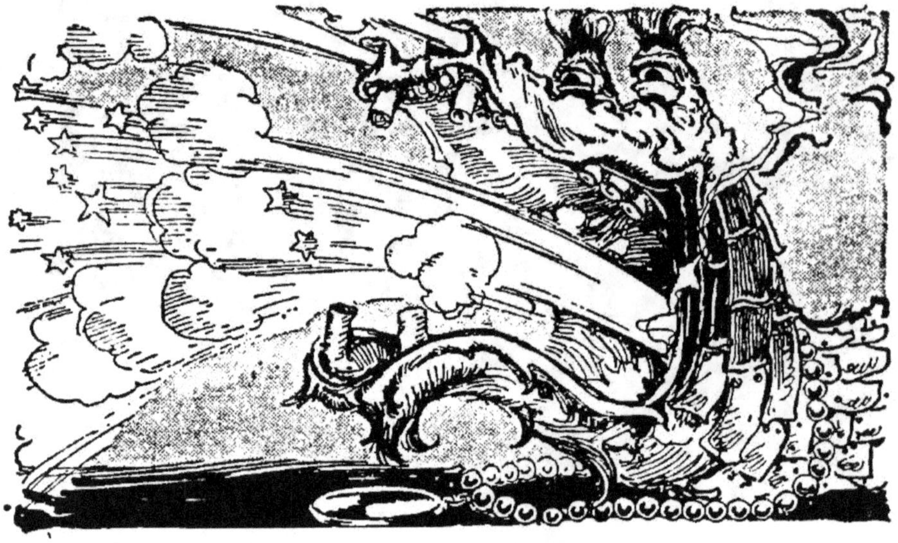

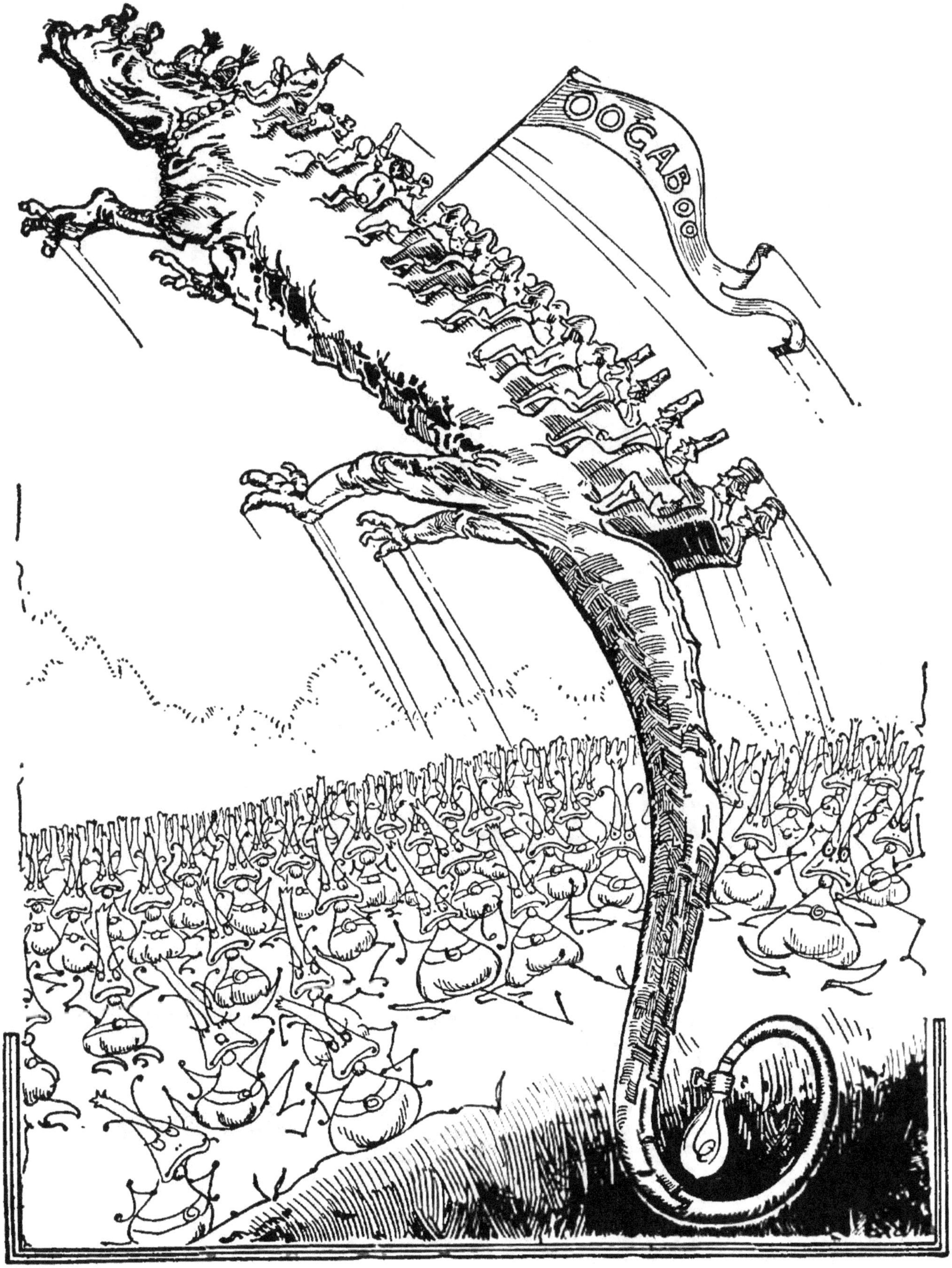
OOGABOO

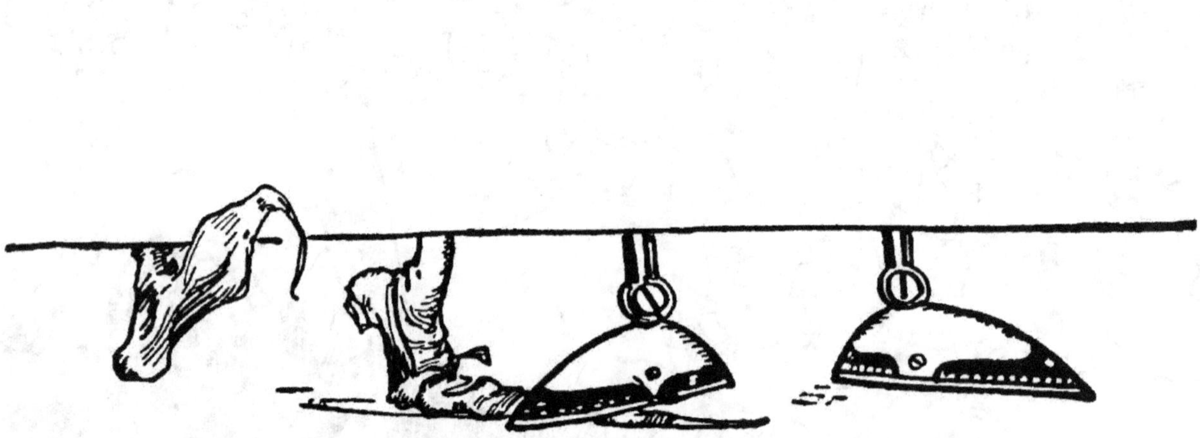

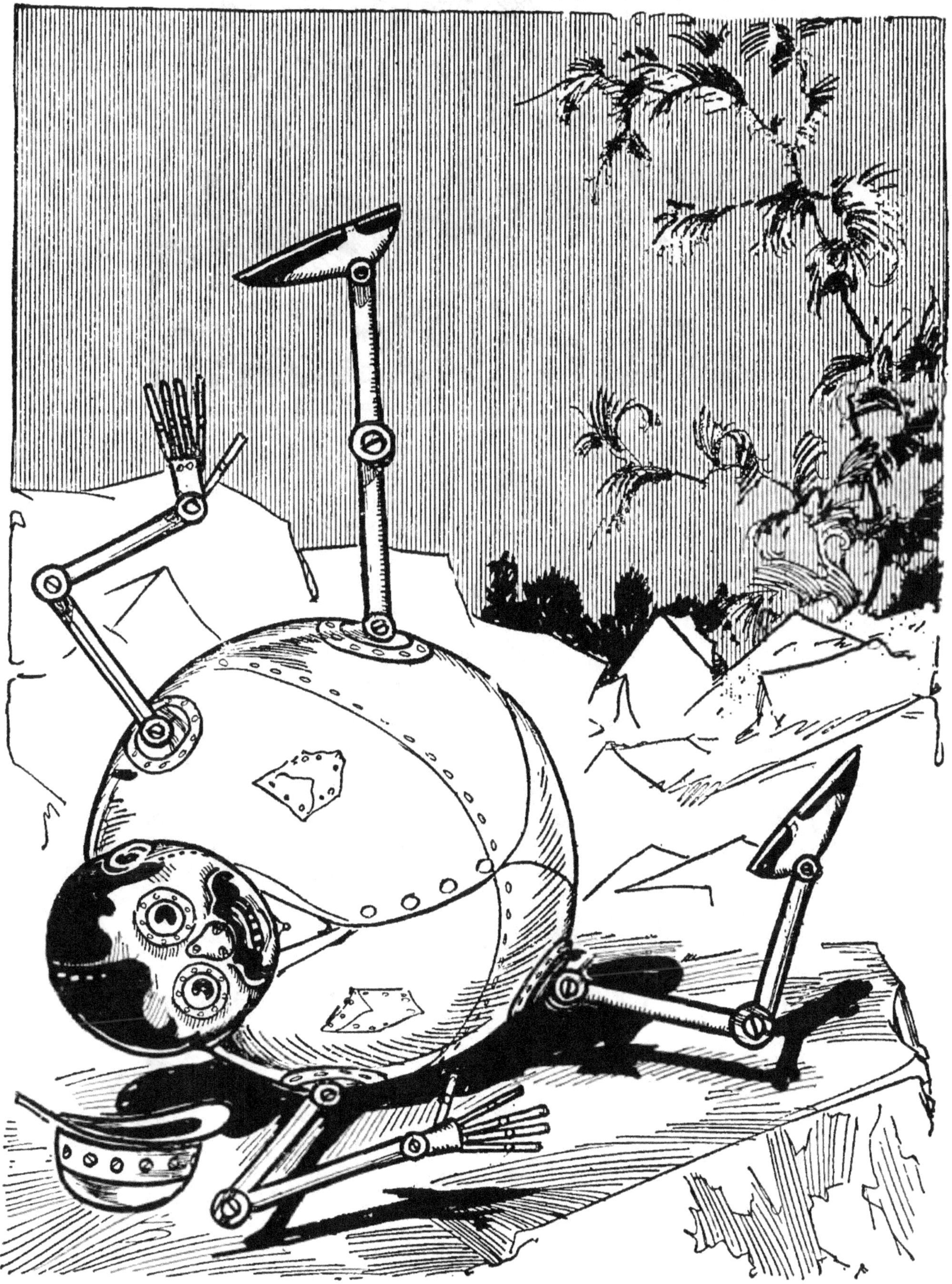

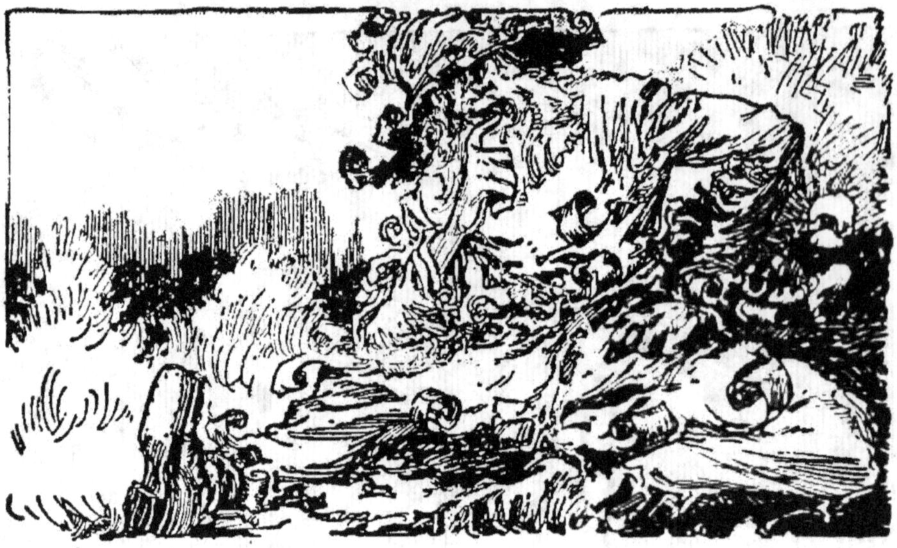

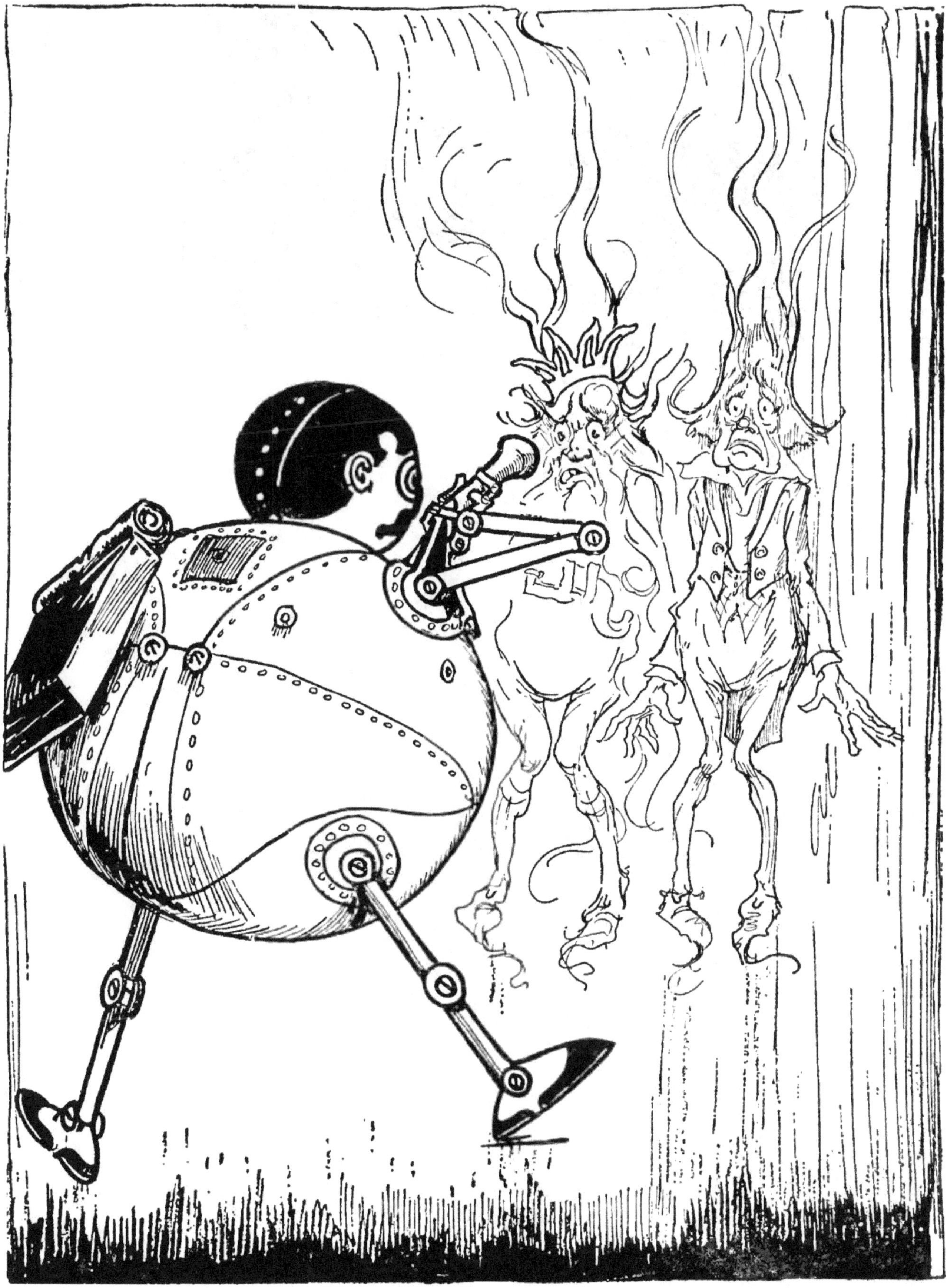

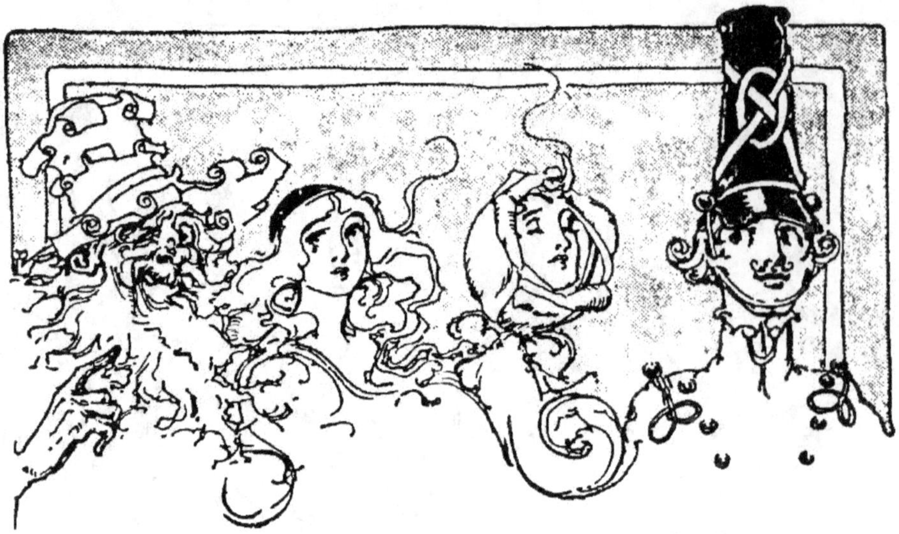

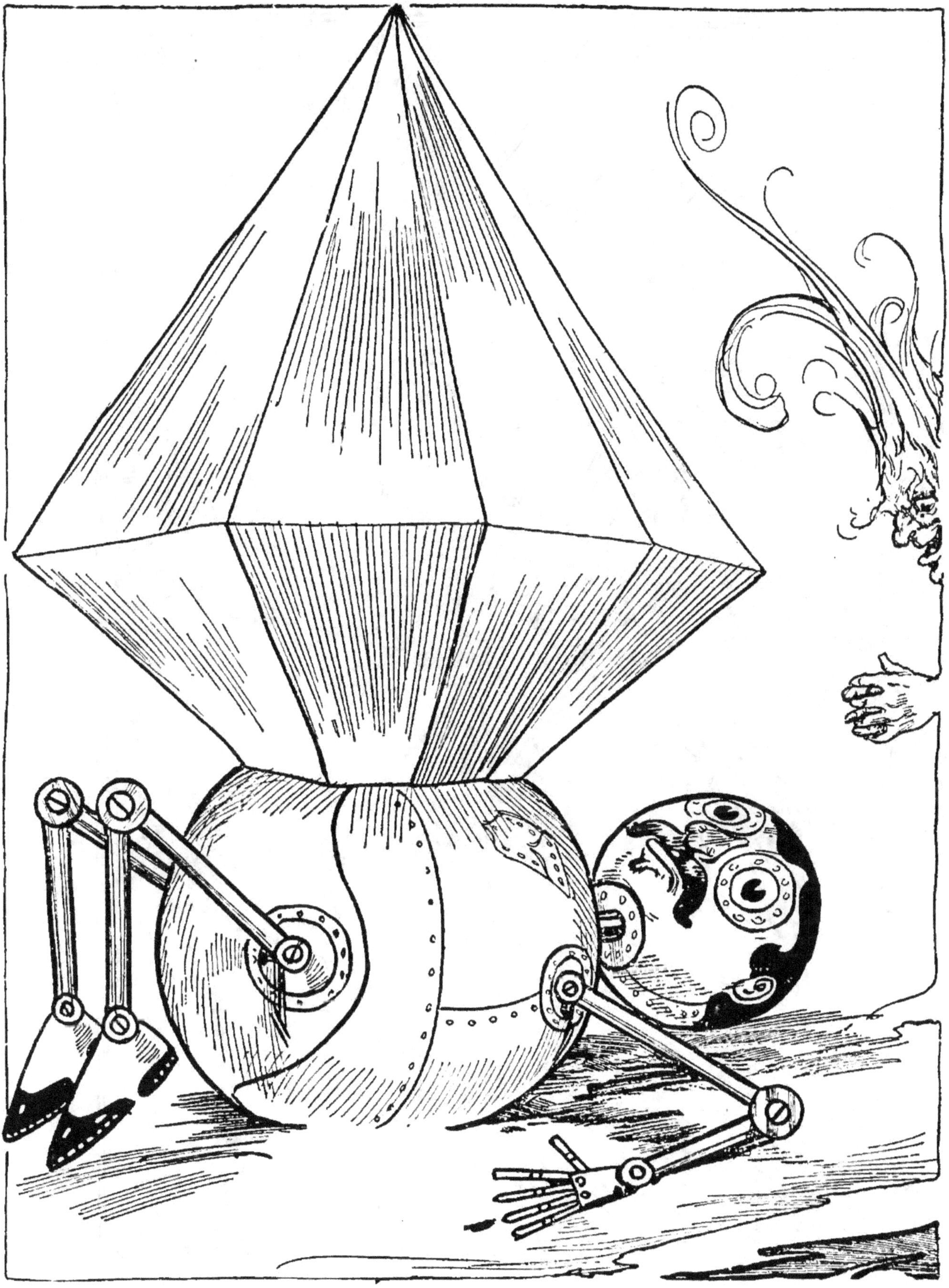

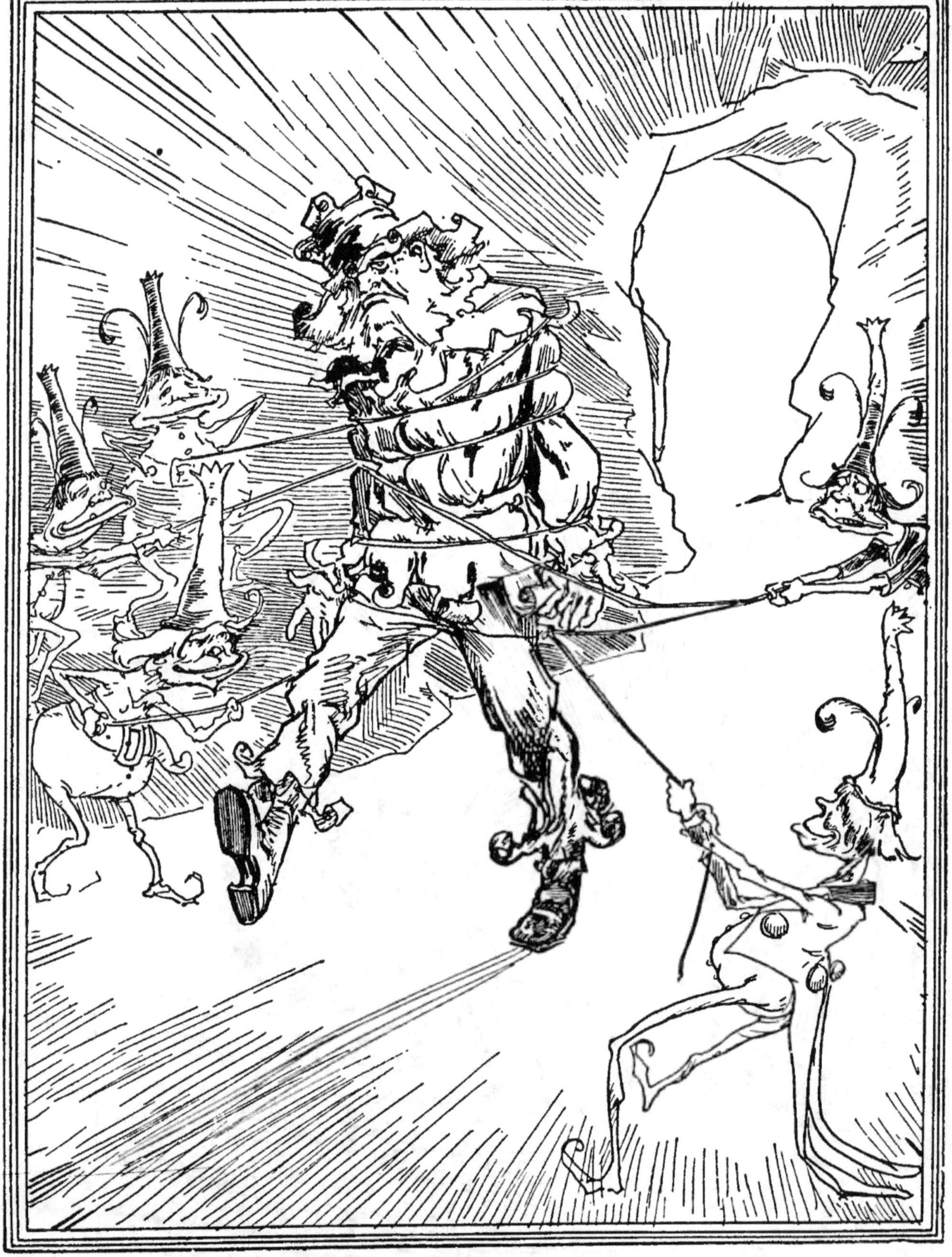

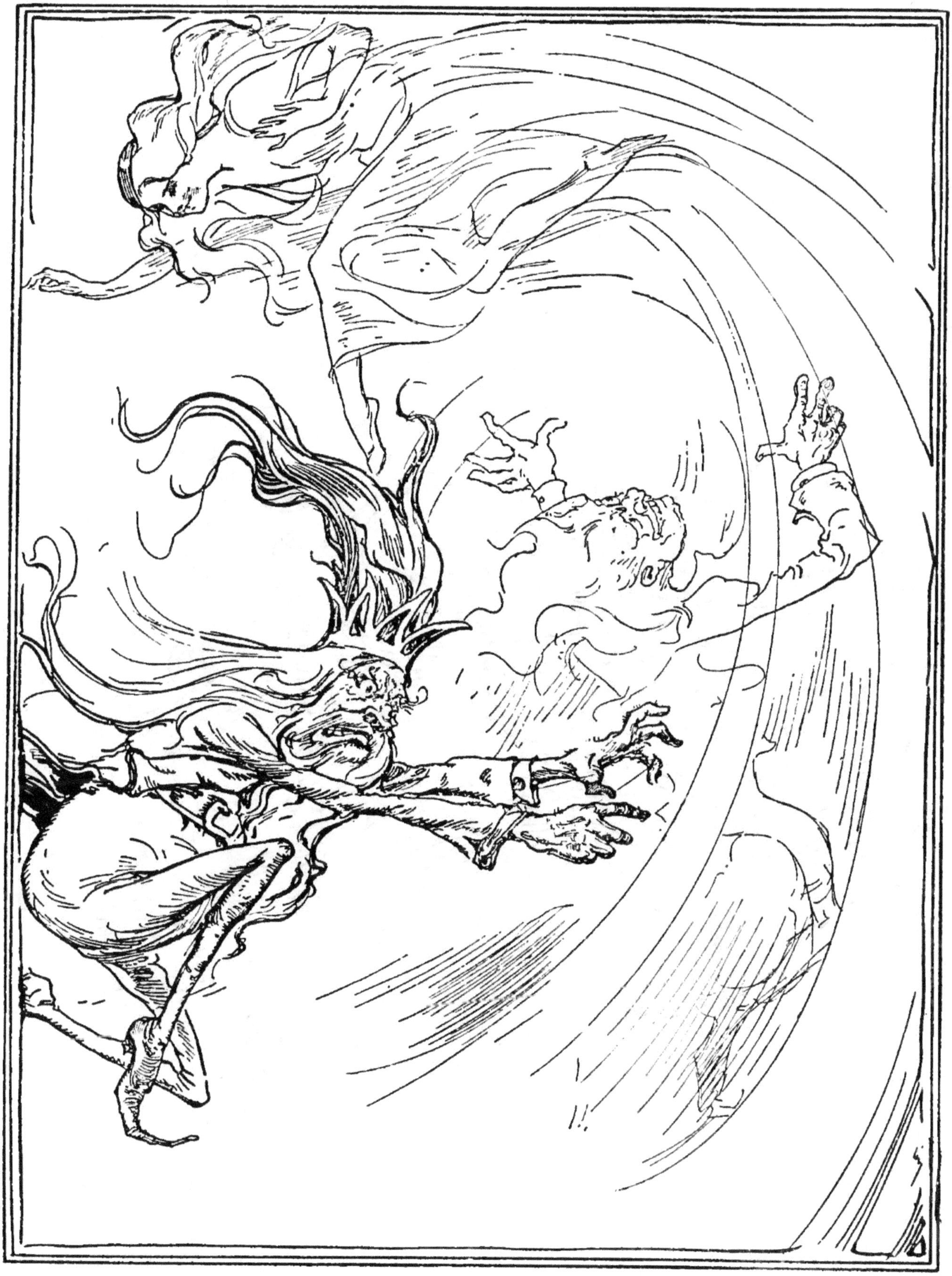

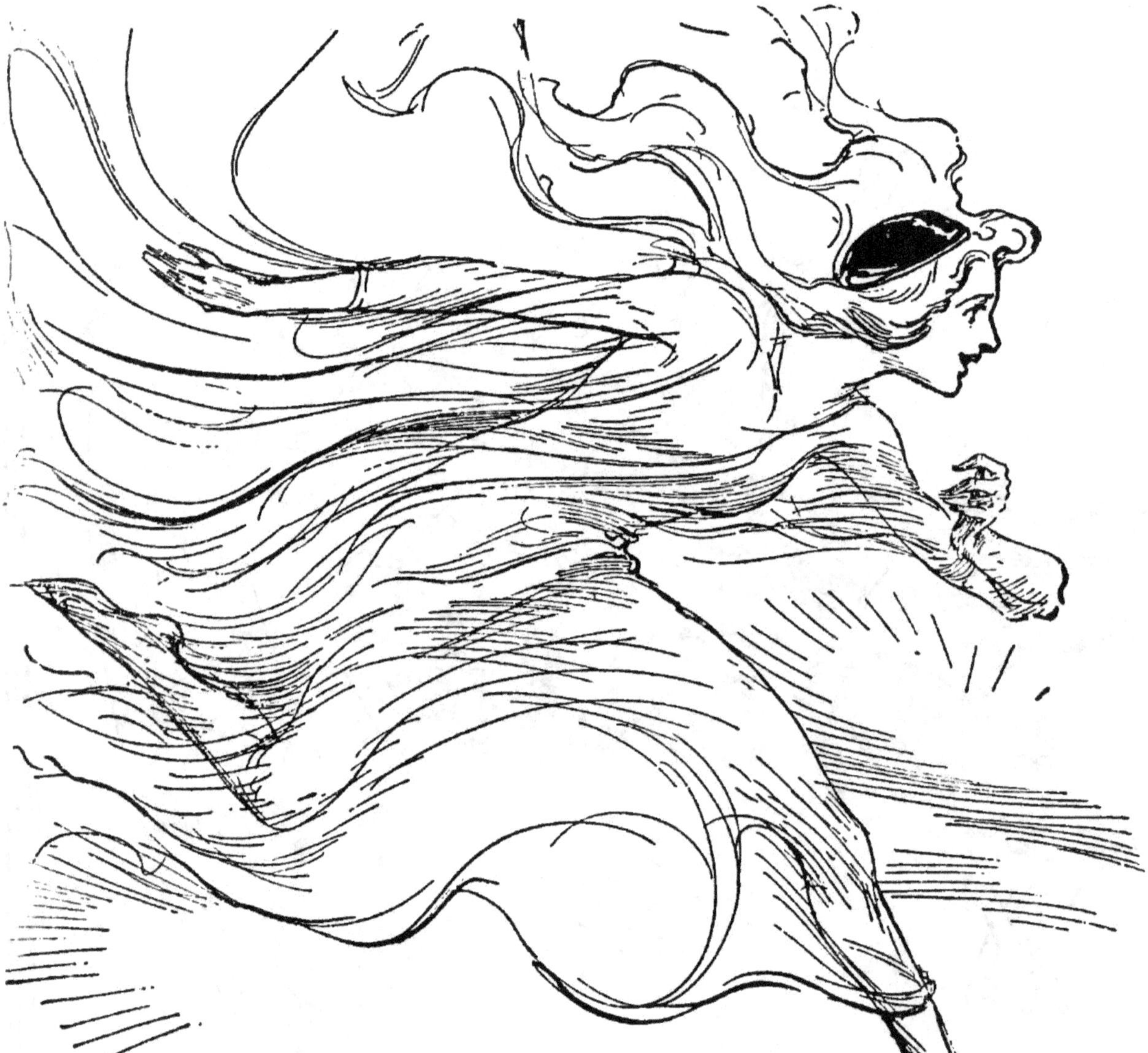

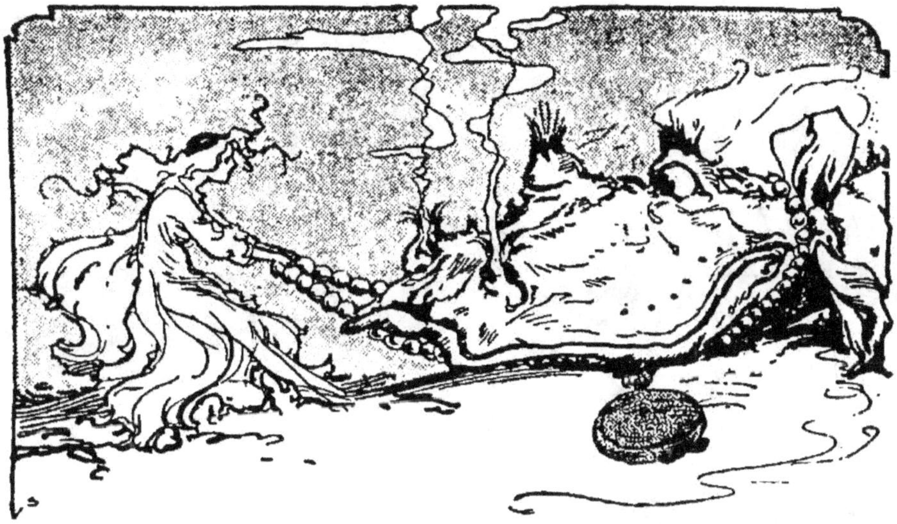

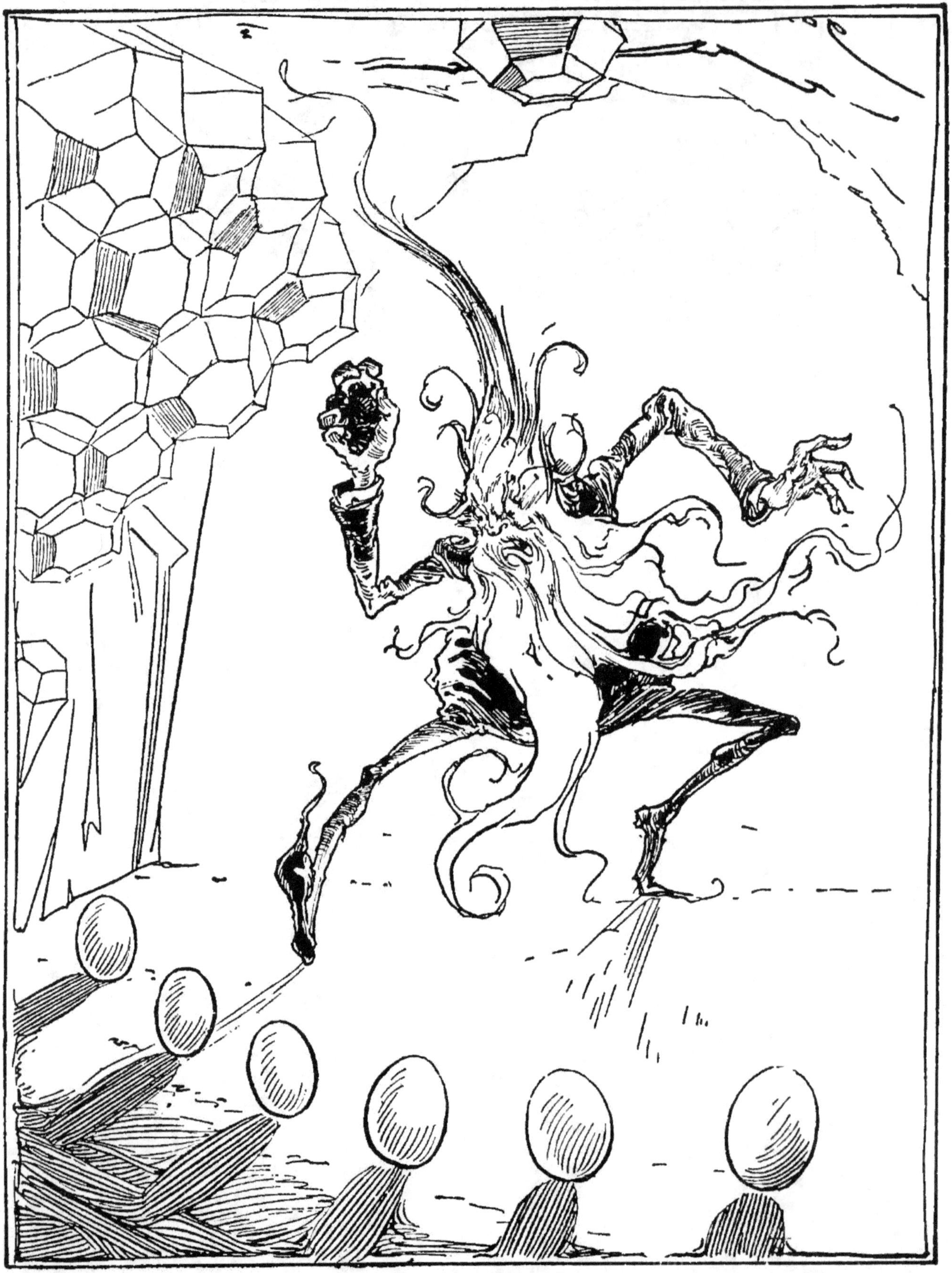

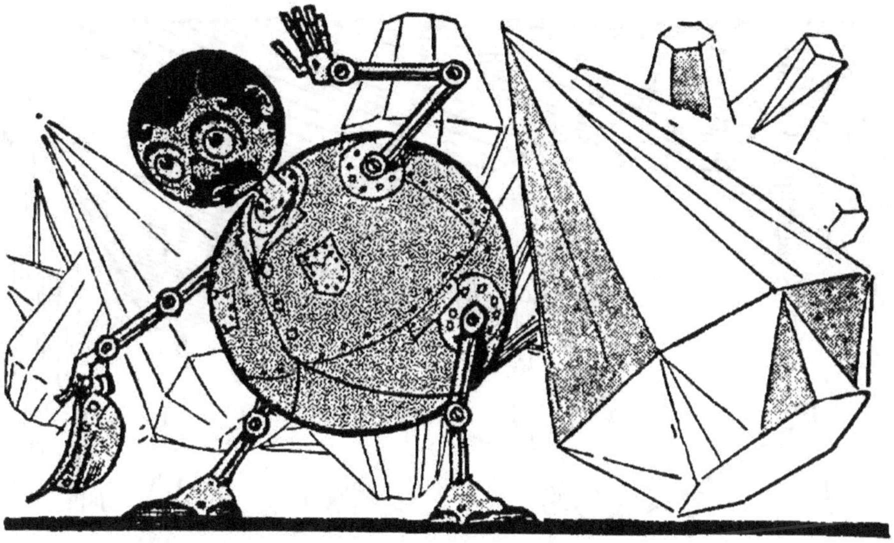

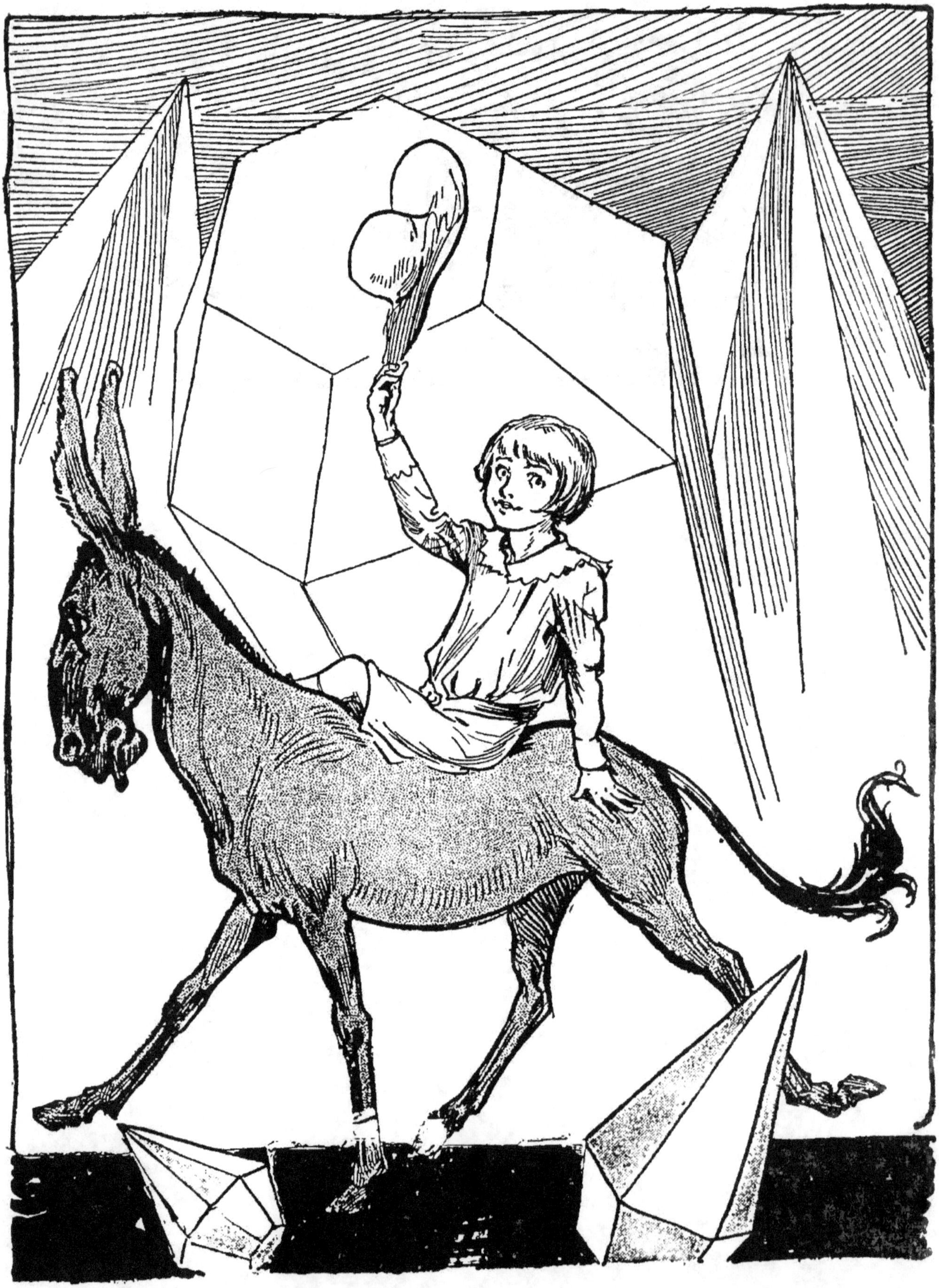

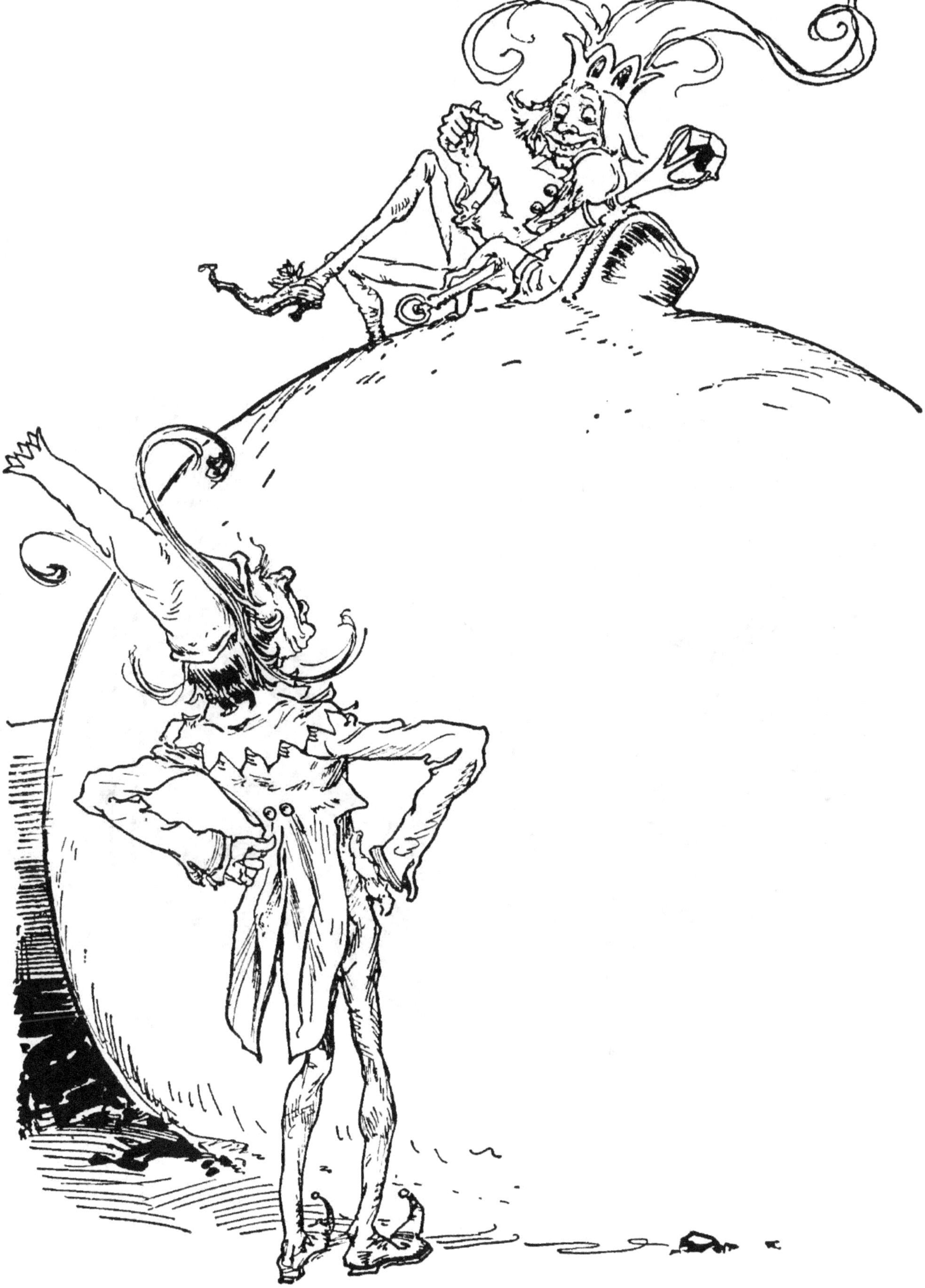

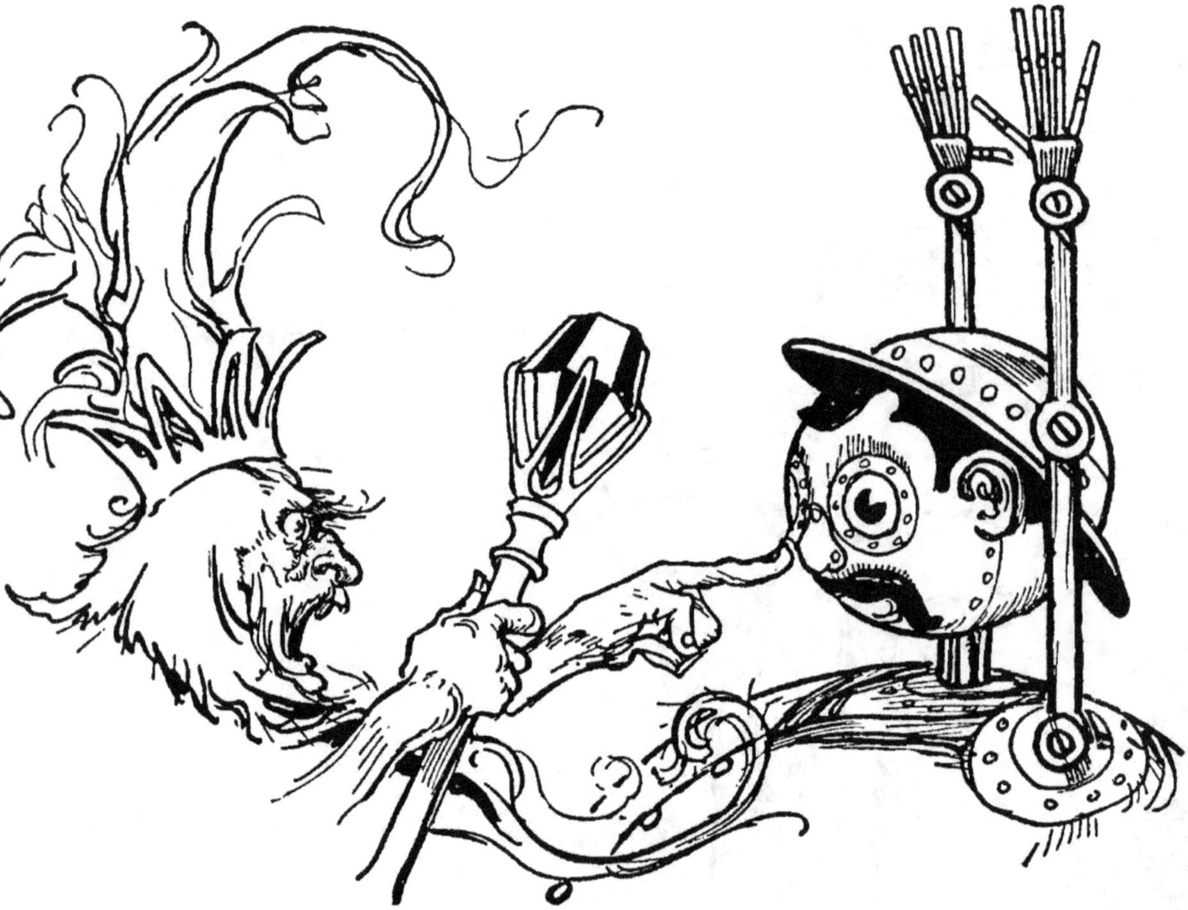

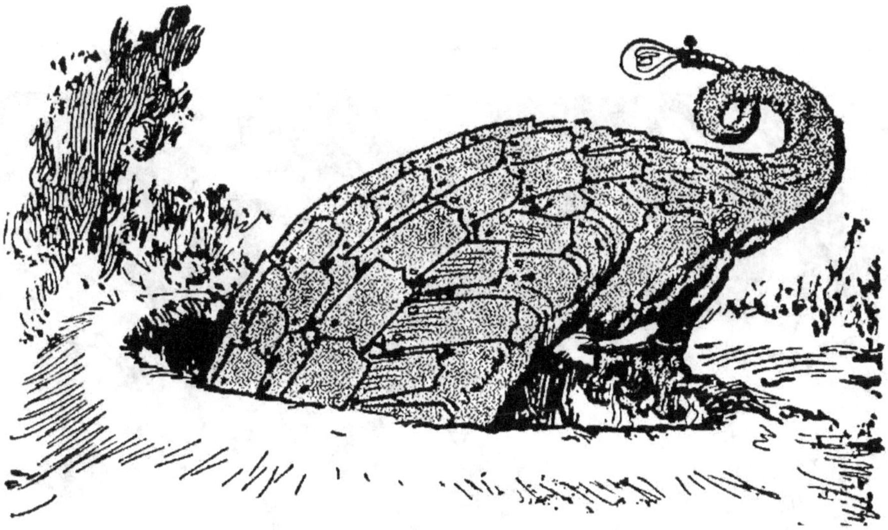

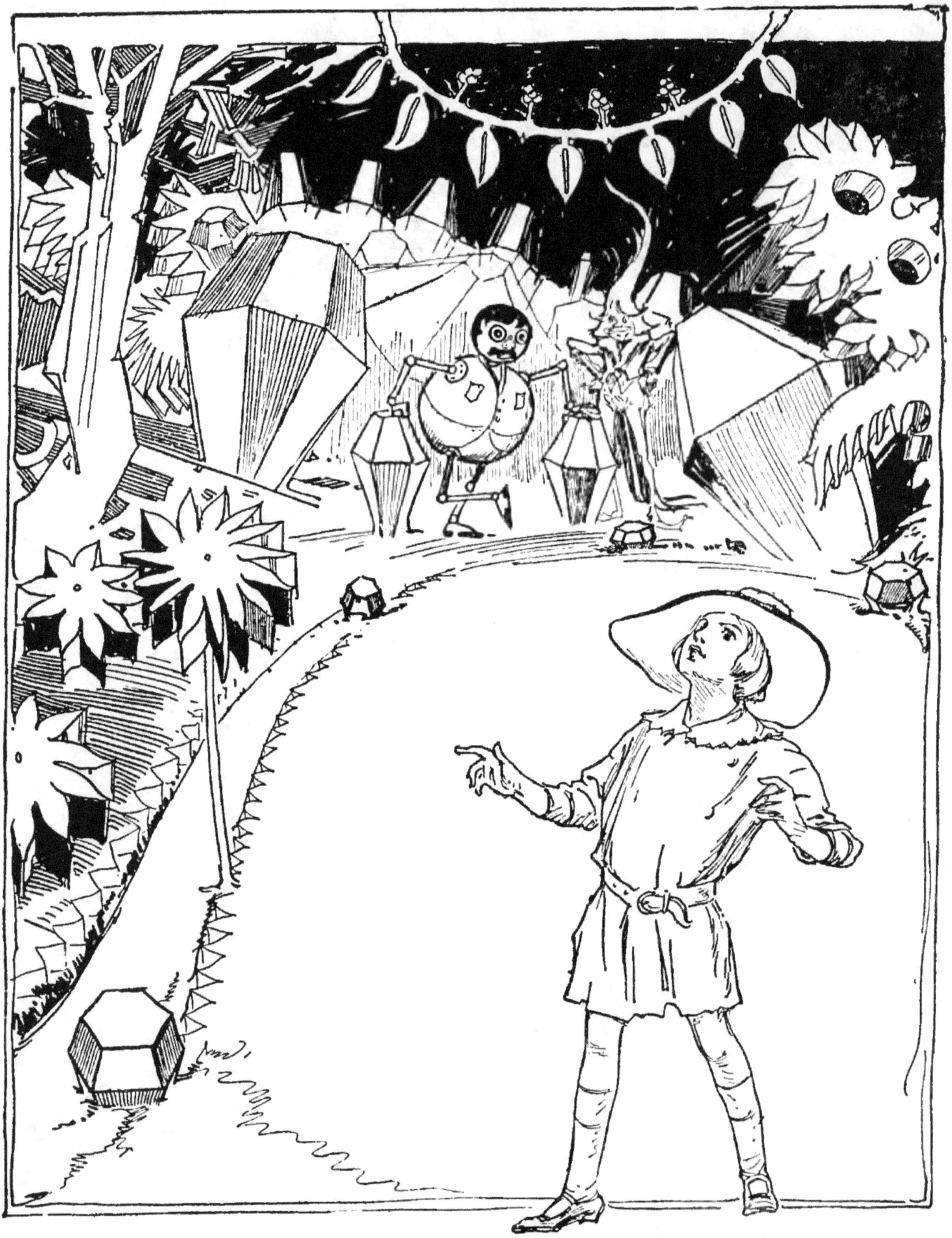

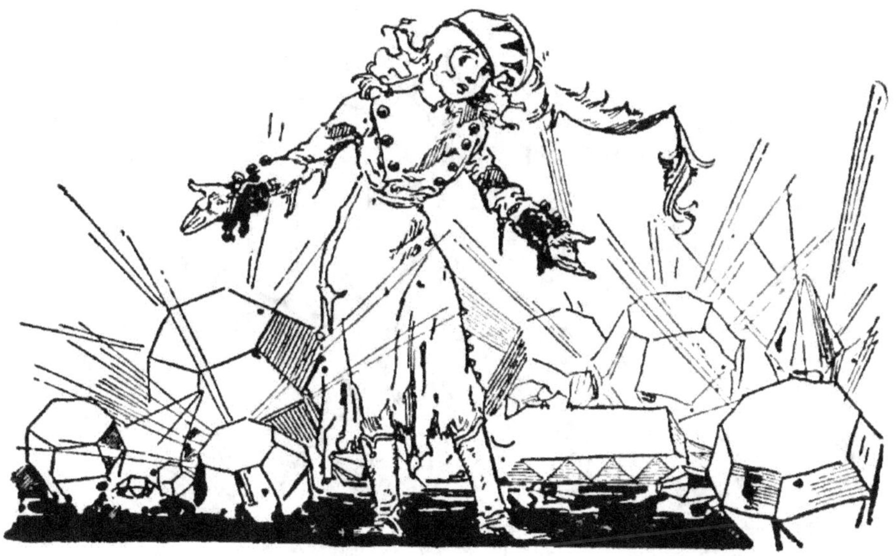

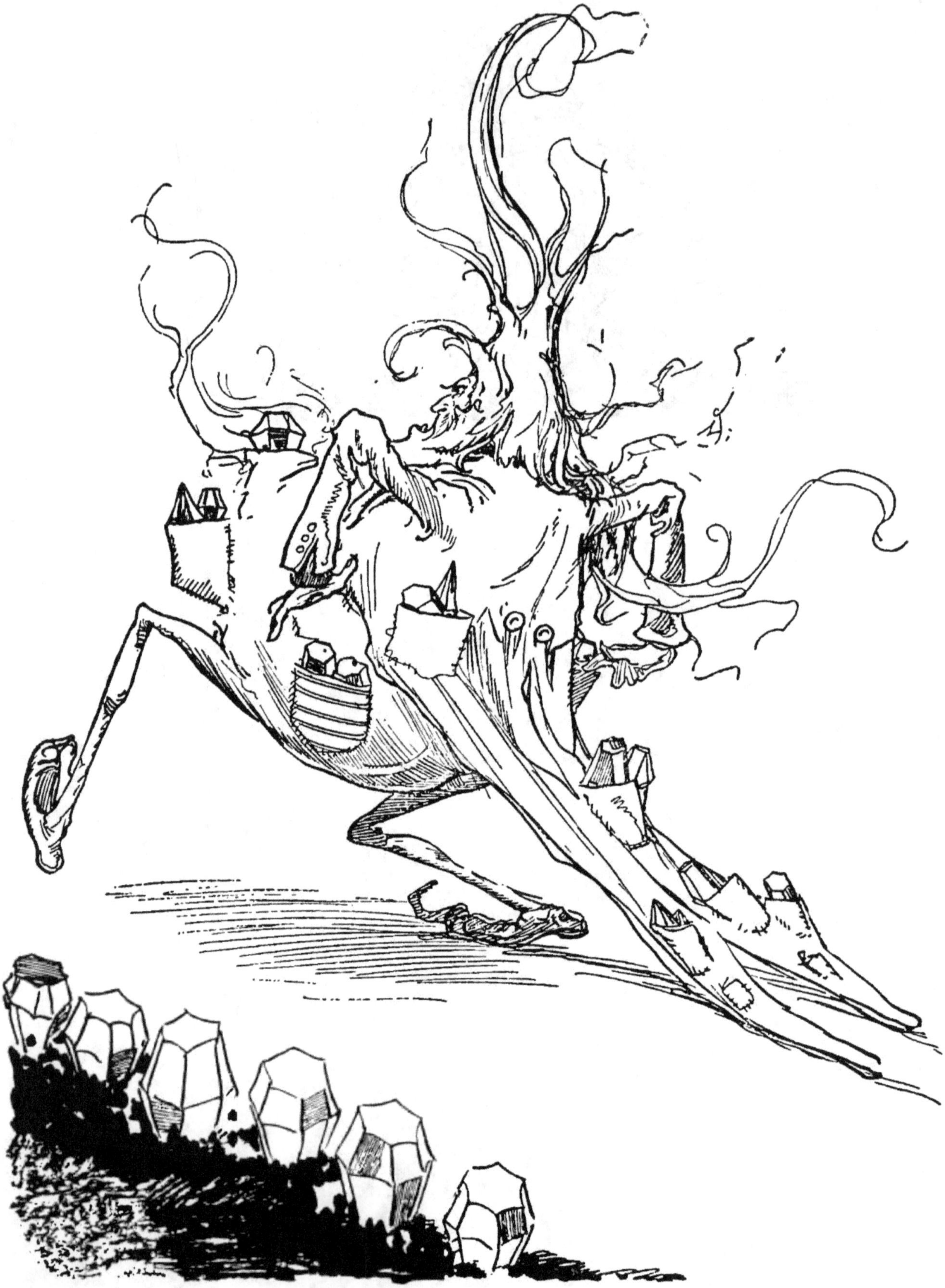

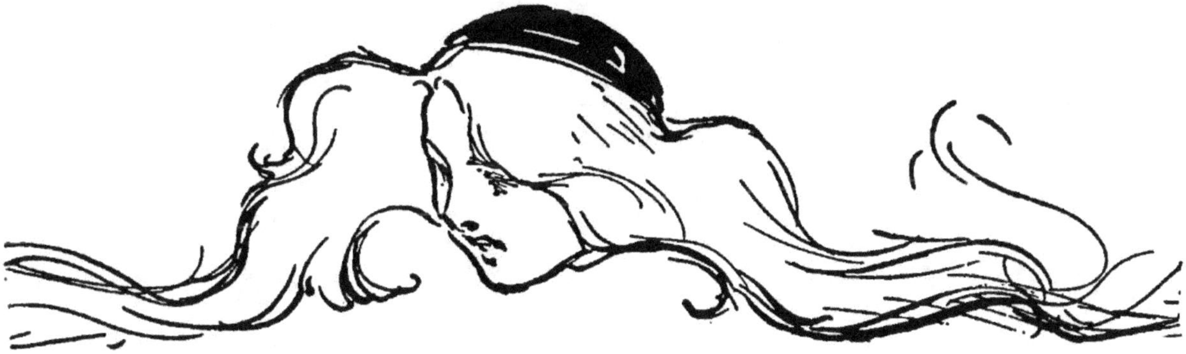

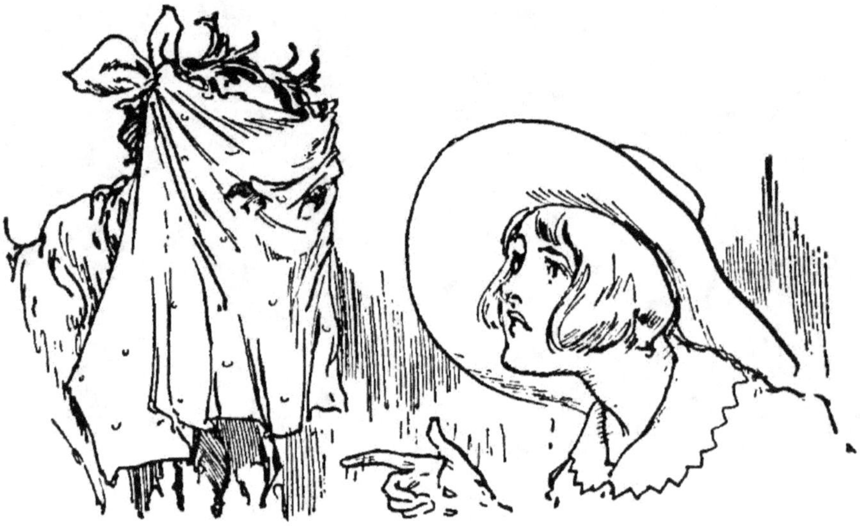

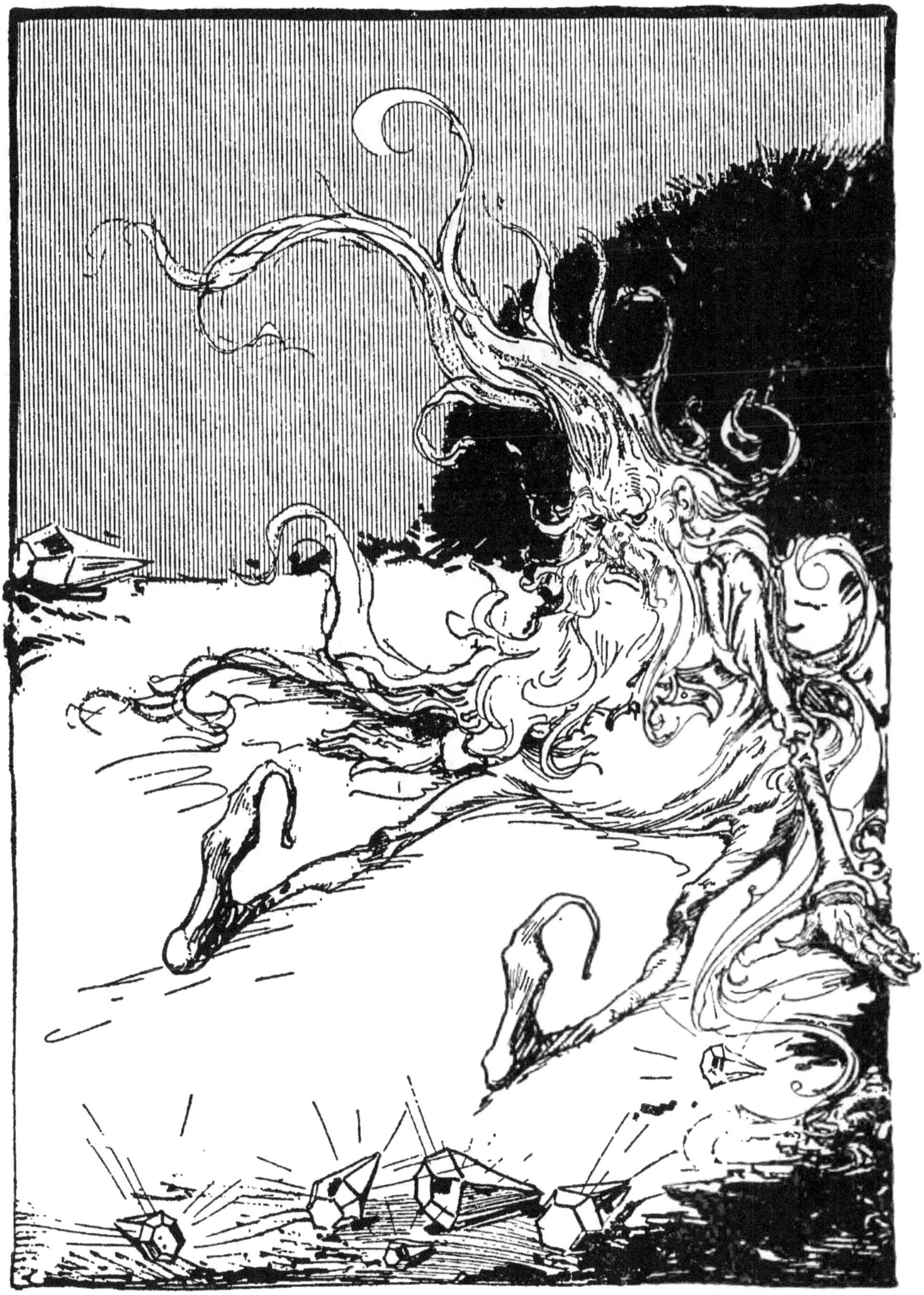

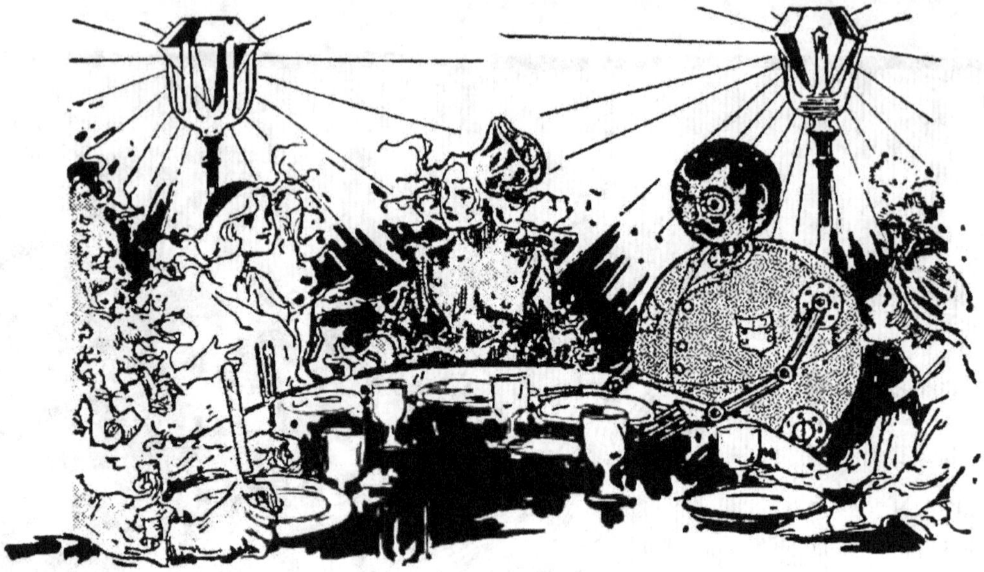

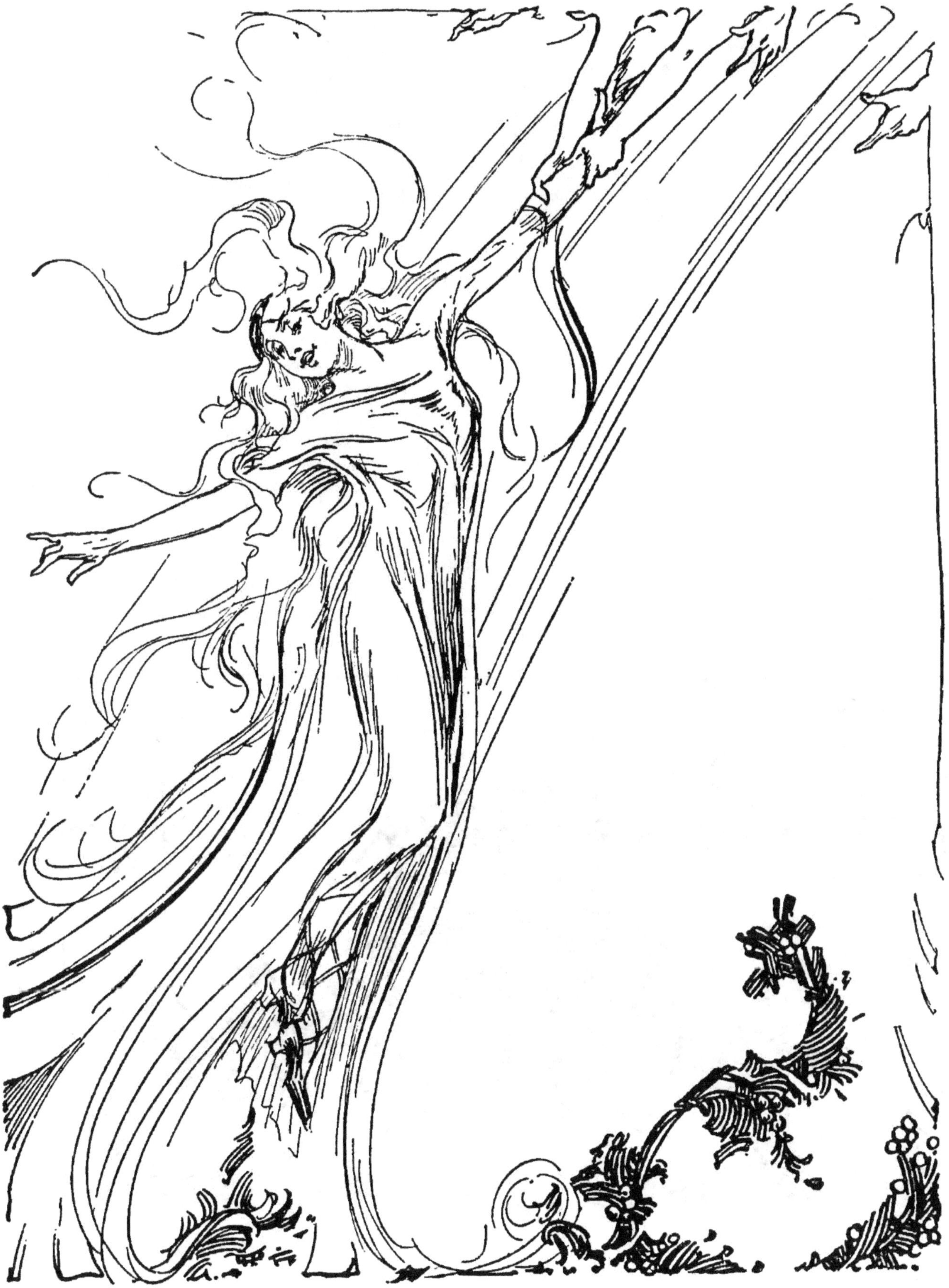

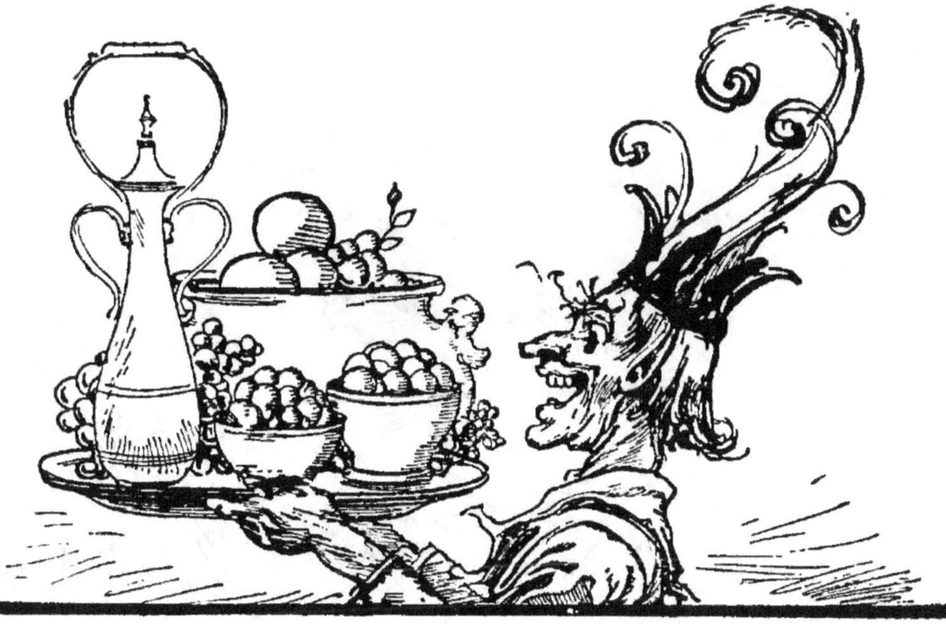

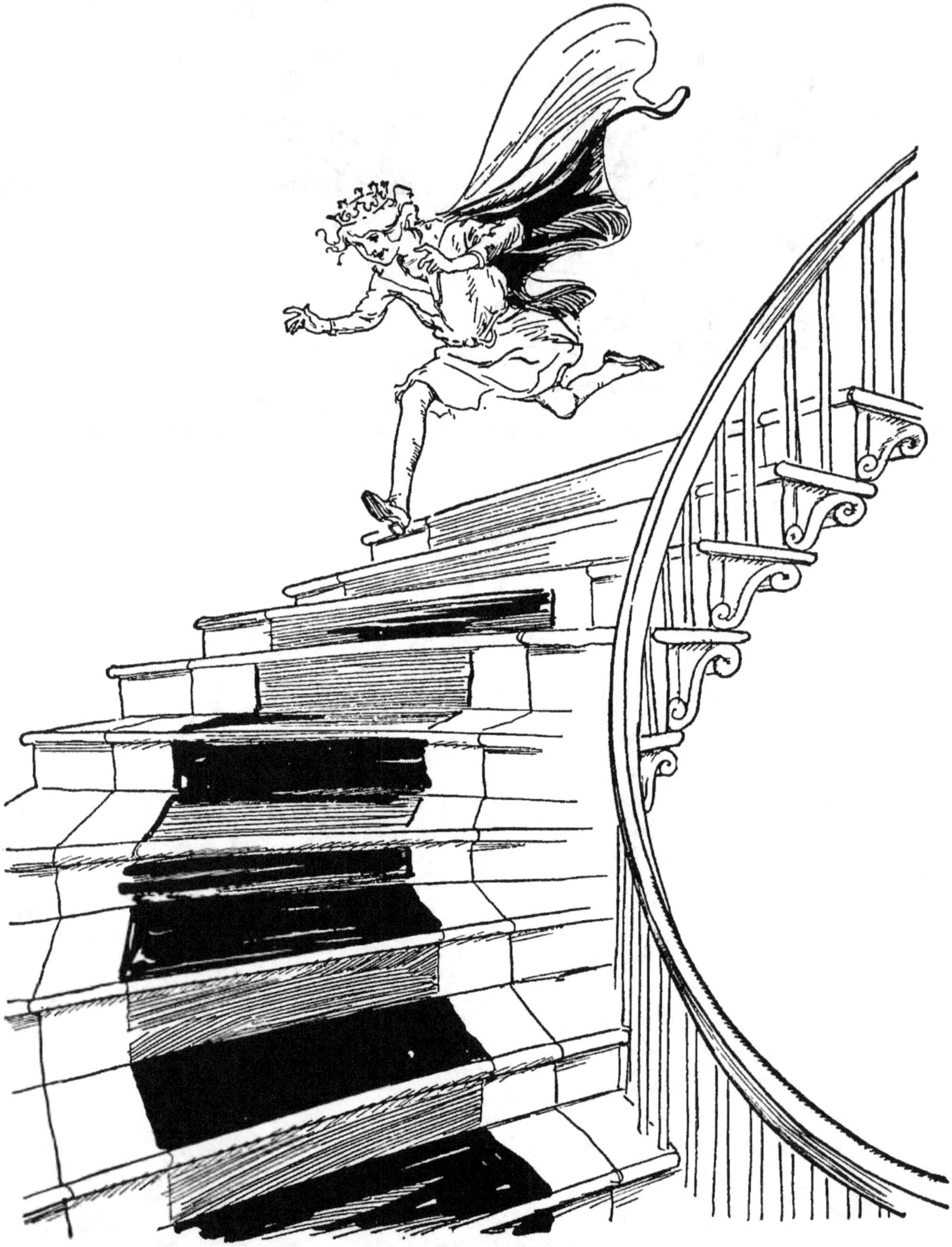

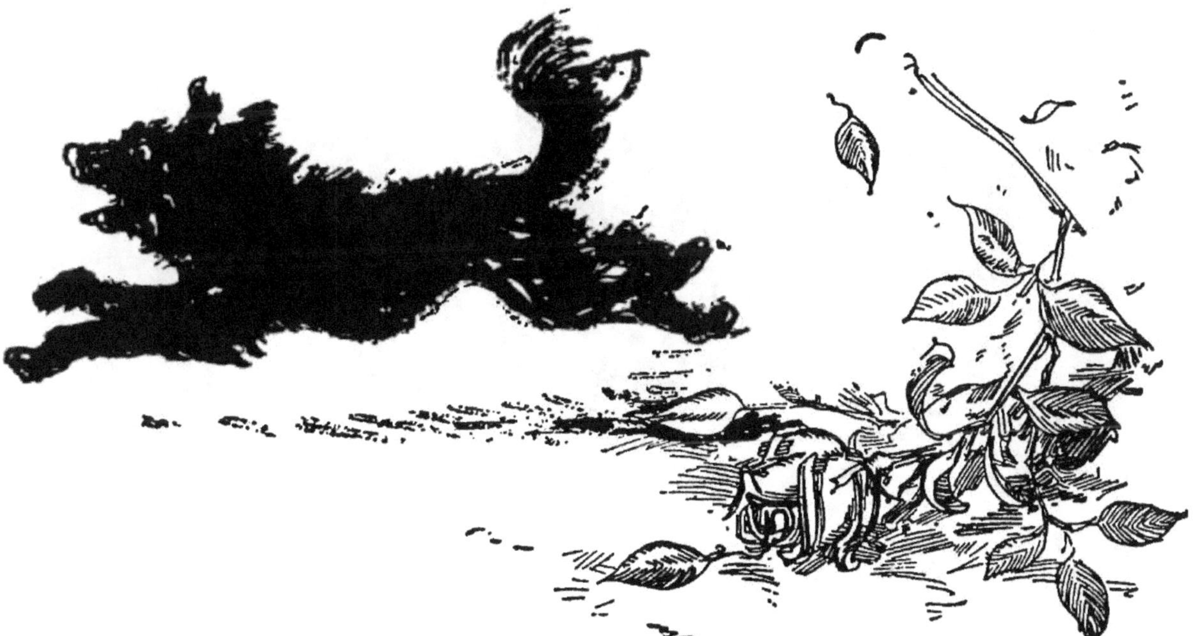

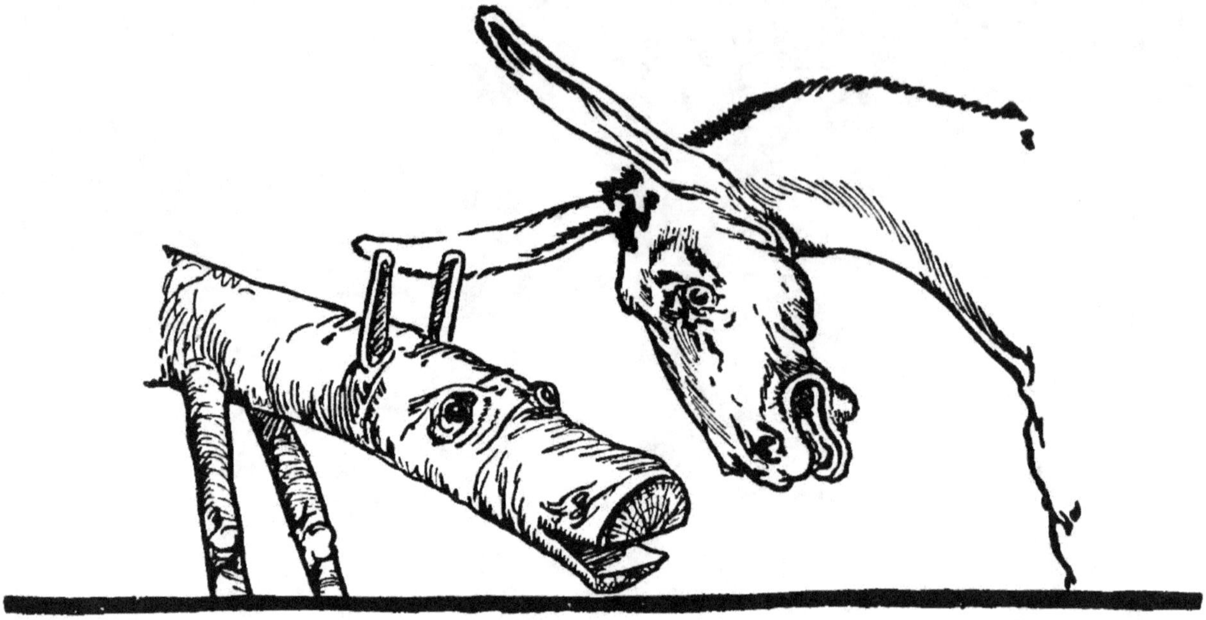

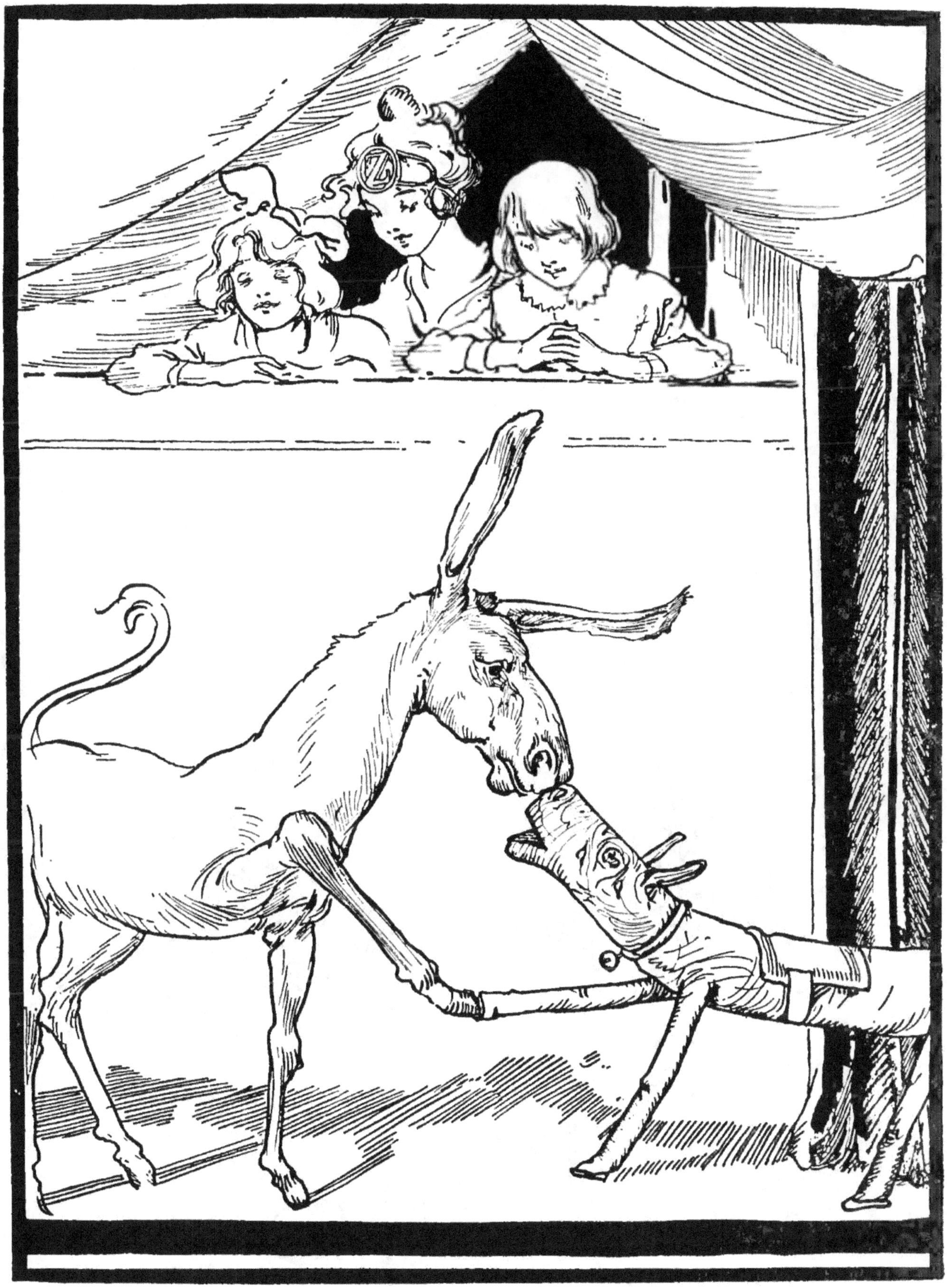

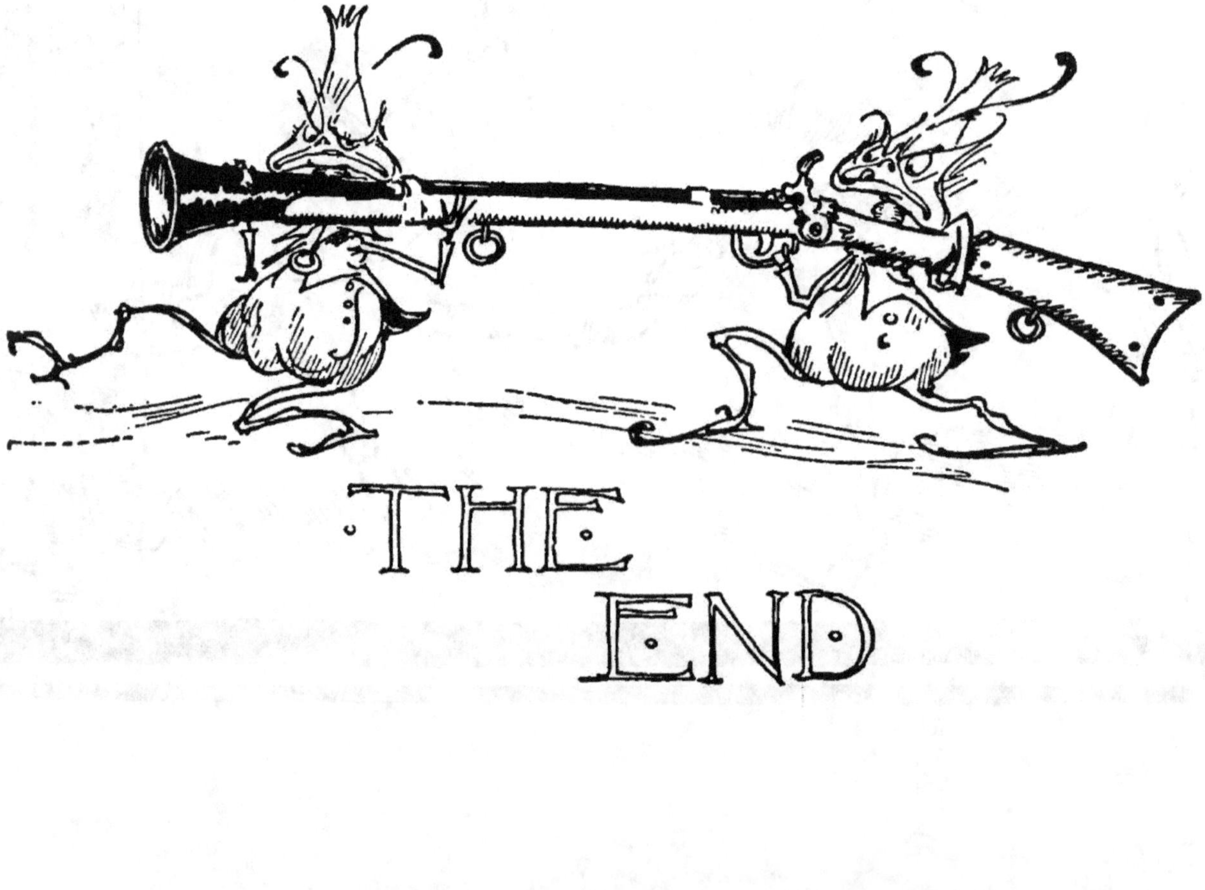
THE END

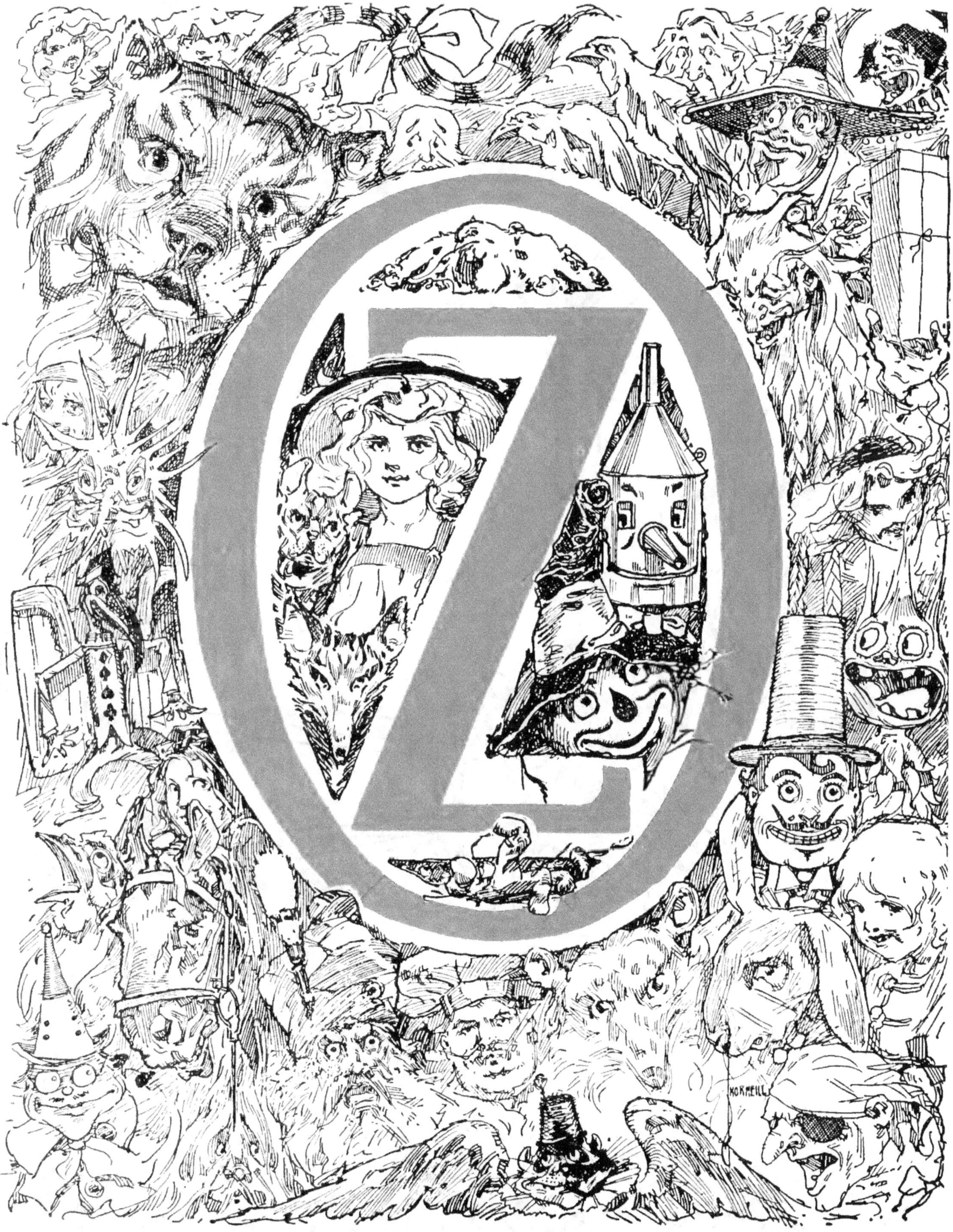
OZ

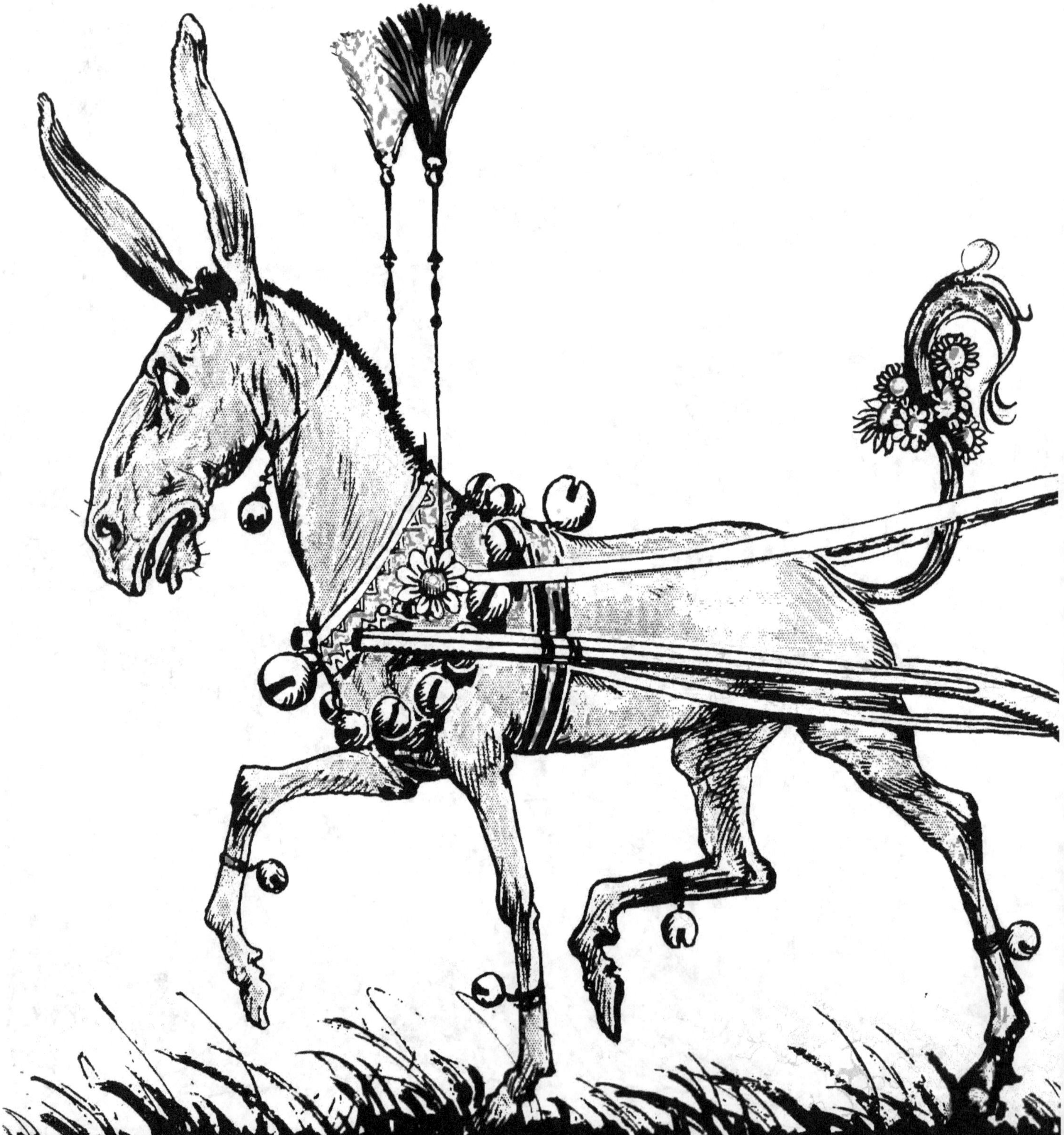

www.ingramcontent.com/pod-product-compliance
Lightning Source LLC
Chambersburg PA
CBHW081119180526
45170CB00008B/2922